"Sumptuously written and accessibly presented, Gloria Furman's *Missional Motherhood* brings the riches of the gospel and the glory of Christ to bear on every mother's work. Her book was like a firm hand of a wise and loving friend, bringing both conviction of sin and a fresh bounty of grace. This book is rich, deep, funny, startling, edifying, encouraging, and God-honoring. It is a book for all women—not just mothers by adoption or childbearing. It shows how being born male and female as image bearers of a holy God matter in all areas of life. In a world awash with gender-neutral language, gender-neutral bathrooms, and and gender-neutral roles, this book is our generation's clarion call that mothering is humble and high women's work, and it matters to God and to the world."

Rosaria Butterfield, Former Professor of English at Syracuse University; author, *The Gospel Comes with a House Key*

"Gloria's words, challenges, and high view of mothering were what my heart knew to be true in the years of my own mothering journey. I enthusiastically endorse this call to us as women to nurture, to create, and to believe God for the glory of the gospel in the lives of those he has placed in our paths. May thousands of women accept Gloria's challenge to be used by God to transform lives for the glory of his kingdom in their homes and in their worlds. Selah!"

Barbara Rainey, Founder and Creator, Ever Thine Home

"With Christ-centered clarity, Gloria shows that our Savior calls us to a grand, global mission to nurture his disciples for his glory. This book is for every re-deemed woman whose mothering heart longs to nurture biological and spiritual children."

Susan Hunt, Former Director of Women's Ministries, PCA; coauthor, *Women's Ministry in the Local Church*

"With a firm grasp of the biblical narrative and a sharp focus on the mission of God, Gloria Furman challenges us to see motherhood as it is—not just a high calling but a part of the mission of God. You'll be encouraged and challenged by this book!"

Ed Stetzer, Billy Graham Distinguished Chair of Church, Mission, and Evangelism, Wheaton College

"Gloria Furman writes from a place of great wisdom and deep trust in Christ, but she also just gets the chaos of it all. She will humbly take you by the hand and help you dream about how to unleash into the world children who actually love Jesus and want to impact their world to do the same."

Jennie Allen, Founder and Visionary, IF:Gathering; author, *Nothing to Prove*

"*Missional Motherhood* is an excellent reminder of my most important job: to teach my children the glorious gospel. Gloria Furman encourages us as moms, amidst all our other responsibilities, to make disciples, starting in our own home. You will be challenged, encouraged, and blessed as you read this beautiful, powerful book."

Heather Platt, mother of four; wife of David Platt, President, International Mission Board

"This is no DIY-perfect-parenting book. The cross looms large over its pages as Gloria swings open the gallery doors of Scripture to show us stunning portraits of Christ and the panorama of his far-reaching redemption. Reading this book made me want to get ahead of the kingdom choir in Revelation 5 and sing with joy, 'Worthy is the Lamb!'"

Tim Keesee, Executive Director, Frontline Missions International; author, *Dispatches from the Front*

"Gloria shows us that motherhood is more about God than about mothering, and that brings me great comfort as I parent four children and disciple other women around me. *Missional Motherhood* is about living, doing, teaching, and talking all about the Word of God and not just how we parent our children in our home. If you are a woman who loves Jesus, this is a book you should devour, regardless of whether or not you are a parent. I can't wait to share this book with all the women in my life!"

Jamie Ivey, host, *The Happy Hour with Jamie Ivey* podcast, JamieIvey.com

"Believing that our biblical theology as moms directs the way we view the mission of motherhood, Gloria takes us through a journey in both marveling at the greatness of God's plan for redemption and embracing the opportunity to make an eternal impact from the everyday context of mothering. *Missional Motherhood* leads weary moms back to the gospel and reminds us that we are investing our lives in what is eternal."

Ruth Chou Simons, artist; author, *GraceLaced*; Founder, GraceLaced Co.

"Gloria Furman does an incredible job of helping mothers rediscover the pattern, promises, and power of Jesus in the midst of everyday life. This book will galvanize you to see and treasure Jesus as the aim and fuel of your everyday mission as you make disciples. So, moms: pour over this book to get a renewed vision for the radically significant mission you've been called to."

Michael "Stew" Stewart, Founding Director, Verge Network and Conferences

Missional Motherhood

The Everyday Ministry of Motherhood
in the Grand Plan of God

Gloria Furman

:: CROSSWAY®

WHEATON, ILLINOIS

Library of Congress Cataloging-in-Publication Data

Names: Furman, Gloria, 1980- author.
Title: Missional motherhood : the everyday ministry of motherhood in the grand plan of God / Gloria Furman.
Description: Wheaton : Crossway, 2016. I Includes bibliographical references and index.
Identifiers: LCCN 2016009734 (print) I LCCN 2016011160 (ebook) I ISBN 9781433552274 (tp : alk. paper) I
    ISBN 9781433552281 (pdf) I ISBN 9781433552298 (mobi) I ISBN 9781433552304 (epub)
Subjects: LCSH: Motherhood—Religious aspects—Christianity. I Mothers—Religious life.
Classification: LCC BV4529.18 .F865 2016 (print) I LCC BV4529.18 (ebook) I DDC 248.8/431—dc23
LC record available at http://lccn.loc.gov/2016009734

Warmly dedicated to
Tiffany James and Tiffany Sumlin,
who missionally mothered college freshman girls
by laboring in prayer, teaching the gospel,
and sharing their very lives.

*Jesus invites women to missional motherhood:
to follow his pattern, to trust his promises, and to nurture
others by the power he provides.*

Contents

Acknowledgments

Books are a community project, and I have many people I want to thank for their help.

To my husband, *Dave*, thank you for everything—for your time and energy, prayers and love. And thank you, *Aliza*, *Norah Claire*, *Judson*, and *Troy*, for inspiring me with your childlike faith and your love for "neighbors who don't know good news yet."

I'm grateful for the influence of my mother, *Catherine*, whose embodiment of hopeful patience is a great encouragement to me.

Several women have shared with me their wisdom, skills, and time, helping to shape the content of this book at every level through personal conversations or manuscript reviewing. This book is far better thanks to *Theresa Barkley*, *Kris Lawrence*, *Angelia Stewart*, *Jenny Davis*, and *Bev Berrus*. Special thanks go to *Karalee Reinke*, whose laser focus on the gospel has sharpened and brightened every page.

I'd like to thank the entire team at Crossway for their enthusiastic support, especially *Justin Taylor*, *Amy Kruis*, *Angie Cheatham*, and *Lydia Brownback*.

Though I doubt that many men imagine that their names would appear in a book with "motherhood" in the title, I owe these particular scholars a debt of gratitude. Through their varied writings they have helped shape my perspective, showing me how biblical theology has everything to do with the meaning and mission of motherhood. I am thankful for the ministries of *G. K. Beale*, *Kevin*

Vanhoozer, Tom Schreiner, D. A. Carson, John Piper, T. Desmond Alexander, Graeme Goldsworthy, and *Geerhardus Vos*.

I could not have started and finished writing this book if it hadn't been for the generous assistance of *Katlyn Griffin* and the encouragement of *Andrew Wolgemuth*. Thank you!

Introduction

What Is This Book About?

You are not "just" a mom.

My mission in writing this book is to show how motherhood is part of the mission of God, thereby banishing, once and for all, the insipid notion that mothering is insignificant. There's no such thing as "just a mom," because there is no mere "just" in the calling of motherhood. That is a wicked lie that is set on fire by hell. You have never met "just" a mother—or "just" a woman, for that matter. I also want to make the case for "every woman mothering" ministry. Every woman is created to nurture (mother) the life that God himself creates. And that is why Satan hates women who mother others.

I realize that talk of banishing things and hell and Satan sounds melodramatic in a preface, but I hope you'll see before the end of chapter 1 all the evidence against the modern scorn and trivialization of motherhood. If you think it sounds like I'm picking a side in a Mommy War, you are right. Ever since the Serpent hissed the first flaming lie into the first woman's ears, we've been at war, struggling against the evil powers and principalities that once held us in sin. There are forces at work in this world that are hell-bent on banishing life, especially life that is created in the image of

God. But now the grace of God has appeared, bringing salvation for all people (Titus 2:11). Satan tries to banish life, but God calls us to nurture life. This book shows that motherhood is mission, in light of Jesus's work in creation, redemption, and his triumph over his enemies.

I want you to know that I'm not against the whimsical aspect of motherhood—not in the least. I've stared at my babies' eyelashes in wonder and wished I could bottle up the sounds, smells, and feelings of certain mommy moments in my memory forever. I know the thrill of hope when a lightbulb turns on in a child or a woman I'm discipling. I lie awake in bed at night, giddy as I dream up things to talk about with my neighbor who is interested in Christianity. The other day my youngest son told his first "knock knock" joke, and you would think that the Red Sox had won the World Series by the volume of cheering in our car. My daughter designed and built a habitat for a caterpillar and a bunch of ladybugs that she caught on vacation, and I took pictures of every angle. A friend wrote to testify of God's faithfulness through her first week of being a mom. I thoroughly enjoy all the heart-pounding thrills of being a mother and a disciple maker. I also appreciate the maternal gravity that helps to ground a family in stability in this sin-sick, crazy world. I'm convinced that the seriously precious moments and exhilarating love of a mother for her children and a woman for her disciples reach new heights when the theological ground underneath is rock solid.

A mother's love is a powerful gift. Hallmark cards agree with me on that one, but where does this gift come from? What kind of gift is it? Why do we experience it? Where is it going? I want to show you in this book that *the everyday ministry of motherhood is part of God's mission.* The nature of our nurture is mission. Motherhood is a gift, because it is a reminder that life is a gift.

God did not create motherhood as "just" a list of to-dos. God did not create motherhood as "just" a sentimental greeting card. God did not create motherhood as a trifling, negligible "just."

"God is a spirit, infinite, eternal, and unchangeable, in his being, wisdom, power, holiness, justice, goodness and truth."[1] Nothing he does or wills could possibly be inconsequential or petty. No woman made in God's image, made for God's mission, could be "just" a mom. Missional motherhood is a strategic ministry designed by God to call people to worship the One who is seated on the throne in heaven.

I'm excited to explain that idea more, because it thrills my heart when I remember it. To think that God has called me to meaningful mission in my motherhood—and that it is all of *grace*—blows me away. This book has one main point in a two-part outline that is held together by an introduction and a conclusion, which are like two bookends. Here's the book's summary in one sentence:

> Jesus invites women to missional motherhood: to follow his pattern, to trust his promises, and to nurture others by the power he provides.

When you unpack a suitcase after a trip, you tend to go straight for what you need right away. Perhaps you go straight for your toothbrush or your medication and leave the dirty laundry for later. You bring out what you need first. So, first, we look at an explanation of why missional motherhood is for every woman (not just biological or adoptive mothers), because *mother* is a verb too. We see in the rest of part 1 the foundation for missional motherhood, which is really just a fly-over retelling of the Big Story with an eye for how God has revealed his missional pattern for motherhood and gives promises regarding his plan.

After that, in part 2, we study the implications of the Big Story for our missional motherhood. In those chapters we look at some of the many ways Christian moms all over the world display God's pattern and claim God's promises as they make Christ's disciples. Lastly, of course, I have a conclusion, which is the second bookend. In "The End of Motherhood" we'll see that "Missional Motherhood Is about a Man."

We're going on a high-flying adventure as we scan the Bible to see God's handiwork in creating and sustaining motherhood for his mission of glorifying himself in all the earth. Recently, I saw a video on YouTube of an eagle being released from the top of the Burj Khalifa, the world's tallest building, with a GoPro camera strapped to its body. The footage they caught from the camera is overwhelming. Soaring on the winds and lifted high over the horizon where the sea meets the sky, angling wings to steer into a new panoramic view of the Arabian Desert, dipping dramatically over the metropolis below—it's all there. I hope that reading this book is kind of like watching that perspective-shaping video.

God has placed each of us in different families, churches, denominations, cities, countries, cultures, and seasons. We've been given strengths and weaknesses, responsibilities and privileges. I'm a mom of four kids, and the good works that God has prepared for me to walk in are being played out in and around an eighth-floor flat in the "old town" neighborhood in Dubai, a diverse city in the Middle East. One of my friends and fellow church members is an older single woman who works in a corporate office, travels a lot, and engages her coworkers in Bible study. Our missional mothering looks different in our contexts, but the source and goal of our ministry is the same. The two of us may be aware of one or two things God is doing in our ministries at any given moment, but only he knows the breadth and depth of his activity in and through us.[2]

I'll explain more in the introduction how this book is for every woman in her everyday ministry, and I do hope that groups of women will read it together. I'm praying that you will find an opportunity to sit down with a cinnamon scone and a dear sister in Christ. If you can only find one, go for the scone. (I'm kidding! Go for the sister.) I'm praying that friends will talk about it using hands-free ear buds during their commute or while sitting on the train on the way to Bible study. I'm praying for the moms sitting cross-legged on the carpet holding each others' babies in order to read this book together in community. I'm praying for the empty nesters who seek a quiet place to read along with a friend. And I'm praying for new moms, who could do as I did when I couldn't fall back to sleep after feeding my babies: read by the glowing light of the headlamp you're wearing on your forehead (best baby shower gift *ever*), and send emails back and forth to your friends who are awake on the other side of the world.

So we've recognized that for every woman who reads this book, there are that many diverse contexts represented among us. As in every conversation, it is always tempting to bring everything back around to yourself. (Oh, how I *loathe* this bad habit of mine! See what I did there?) For every time that I talk about my own particular context in this book, I want to be stringently committed to making sure that any exhortation I give to you springs up out of the text of God's word. Heaven knows that what you *don't* need is a book full of my quirky, half-baked how-tos that only work a pathetic percentage of the time. This book is not a catalog of my creative ideas for living missionally—I believe those creative ideas are going to be generated in your own heart as the Spirit strengthens your faith and leads your family.

The aim in *Missional Motherhood* is to give you laser focus on what God's word says about his mission, how motherhood fits in to that, and what Christ has done to fuel and fulfill our everyday ministry as moms. As far as personal application, I'm praying that the Lord will do his work, so you can see the application he has for your life. On every page, the personal application is there for the taking as you ask yourself: "What does God's mission mean for *my own life*? What does this mean for *our lives*, as sisters who are members of one another in Christ's body?" In this particular book I think it will be helpful to think about specific application for missional motherhood in terms of "head, heart, hand, and mouth":

- How does this truth *renew my mind* in the truth? Do I need to change my mind about God, his mission, the gospel, motherhood, my mission, or something else?

- How does this truth *thrill my heart* to love Jesus? Are there affections in my heart that he needs to replace?
- How does this truth *strengthen my hands* for the sacrificial service of nurturing others? How is the Lord leading me to serve?
- How does this truth *open my mouth* to share the good news? What would God have me say to the disciples and the nonbelievers around me?

Let's ask for God's help as we discover the breathtaking virtue of Jesus Christ and the mission he has designed for our mothering.

Part 1

MOTHERHOOD IN THE GRAND PLAN OF GOD

Nurturing Life in the Face of Death

1

Mother Is a Verb Too

I was fired from my first job after only one week. The details are a little fuzzy in my own memory, so I have to rely on my parents to sort out the facts for me. I was, after all, still in elementary school. Reading is my favorite pastime, and my obsession with the written word developed early. When I was in elementary school, one of my teachers took notice. My teacher thought my zeal and skills would be an encouragement to some children in my class who were behind in reading, so she paired me up to help a few of my classmates.

The arrangement didn't last long. My disappointed teacher explained to my parents that while their daughter loved to read, little Gloria lacked the patience to bring other children along with her. I don't remember my feelings being hurt when I was "fired" though. Not having to spend my precious reading time tutoring other kids in reading didn't seem like a loss.

My teacher was right. I had no patience to nurture others, because I believed that serving others and sacrificing my reading time was a loss. I probably didn't articulate it quite like that, though, and can imagine eight-year-old me rolling my eyes and groaning, "Ugh. Do I *have* to?" There's an age-old adage that says, "The world doesn't revolve around you." But from the day we are born until the day we die, that's the story we all prefer to live, isn't it?

The Real Story

If one of my children was about to be mauled by a bear, I would fight the bear without hesitating. That's how fiercely this mama bear loves her cubs. So why do I have to fight off feelings of selfishness when I discover that one of my kids ate the last piece of my birthday cake? It's funny (as in lame, not laughable) how to this day I still struggle with the same self-centeredness that I dealt with when I was an eight-year-old. That knowledge is a gift indeed. God has been so kind and patient toward me for all these years.

So why do we love the people in our lives with passion yet serve them with hesitation? There is a war going on inside us. The fairy tale has been exposed as a farce. We've been alive long enough to know the world doesn't revolve around us, but we sure do prefer the script that says we're the leading lady. If we're going to understand the mission of our motherhood, we need to know the *real* story.

The real story of my life is that I once was lost and now I'm found. God powerfully converted me as a freshman in university. He raised my lifeless soul from the dead, removed my heart of stone, and gave me a new heart of flesh that is prone to love him. Now, I must use precise words to communicate what really happened, for God converted me *to Christ*, not to an idea of "biblical womanhood." My salvation was not determined by *my* faithfulness to live out my God-given femininity but rather by *God's* faithfulness to save me through Christ's work on the cross. As we'll see later from Scripture, Jesus designed womanhood for himself, creating female image bearers in his likeness to faithfully follow him. I gladly affirm and celebrate God's design for women as he has communicated in his word. In my ethnically diverse church, I enjoy watching women from over seventy nationalities live out their God-given design and mission to nurture others. I can hear these friends from Redeemer

Church of Dubai all agree in their beautiful accents that there is no singular culture or solitary superwoman who embodies the godliest epitome of womanly perfection. Jesus Christ alone is the focus, hope, and help of every woman everywhere!

The Bible is full of truth that lands in the living rooms of ordinary people. So it is in that vein that I want to share a little bit more of where I'm coming from (besides my "you're fired" story from the third grade). My husband, Dave, is a man who loves the Lord and is committed to living out the mission Jesus has given him. When we were first married, we were young and strong; nothing could slow us down. In a lot of ways, I didn't need to exercise patience toward my husband or care for him sacrificially. We were quite capable of caring for ourselves, and at times I struggled to keep up with him! When we were both in seminary I was feverishly nervous about the idea of becoming a mother in the future. "We're going to wait five years," was the line my husband and I gave people when they asked about our family-growing plan.

However, five years approached quickly. As the time passed in increments of full course loads and a dozen short-term mission trips, my heart warmed to the idea of becoming a mother. I soon learned from an older woman in my life that my anxiety in this area was not excluded from the "1 Peter 5:7 Rule."[3] We spent nearly two years "trying" before our first child was conceived, and every month I went through a cycle of mixed emotions: from hope, to disappointment, to relief. In those days God taught me a lot about his sovereignty and his kindness. Then, on the evening our first child was born, uncertainty hit me like a tsunami. As I finished feeding my daughter for the first time, the nurse nonchalantly reminded me, "All right, dear; now set your alarm to wake her in two hours to feed her again." *Again?* Exhausted like I had never been before, I could not compose any verbose or eloquent prayers. I simply needed daily bread: "Father, I have no idea what I'm doing. Give me *whatever it is that I need* to do what you've given me to do."

Now, years later, my lack of patience still appears in the way I love my husband who has developed a nerve disease and an accompanying physical handicap. My selfishness appears in the way I nurture my four young children. My self-centeredness appears in the way I relate to my friends at church and fulfill my commitment to love them as brothers and sisters in Christ. It appears in the way I pray for my neighbors and witness to them.

But. Praise the Lord! I don't have to hide behind the "I'm just too busy thinking about myself to serve others; you'll have to find somebody else" narrative. The gospel tells sinful, broken me that I'm actually part of a different story. *Jesus invites women to missional motherhood: to follow his pattern, to trust his promises, and to nurture others by the power he provides.* Jesus Christ is on a mission that he will most assuredly accomplish, and he invites us to participate to the praise of his glorious grace.

Very Vital Verbiage

Have you ever asked a temper-tantruming toddler to "use their words"? Me too. When we talk about theology and motherhood, we not only need to use our words; we need to use the right words. We need to be intentional when we use our words, especially words about who Jesus is and what he is doing. But we also need to be intentional when we use words for motherhood. When I say "mother," I want you to think of it as a verb too. When you read the word *nurture*, I want you to remember everything that it involves: discipling, serving, caregiving, mothering, teaching, showing hospitality, and more.

Mothering (or nurturing) is a calling not just for women who have biological or adopted children. Mothering is a calling for all women. Every Christian woman is called to the spiritual motherhood of making disciples of all nations. Our nurturing is, by nature, *missional*. In this book we'll see how our maternal instinct needs to be conformed to the shape of the cross, and how Jesus himself does this in our hearts from the inside out.

Maybe those words make the mantle of your many responsibilities feel a bit heavier: caring for an ailing parent, counseling a new friend at church, worrying about a wayward son, encouraging your weary husband, serving your suffering neighbor, or praying for a struggling missionary.

When I think about my role in nurturing those around me (and those neighbors who are on the other side of the world), I can feel my proud back being bent beyond its capacity. *Yes, Lord, break our pride and cultivate in us humble hearts as we sacrificially mother our children, minister to our friends, and reach the lost.*

Our faith needs to be strengthened with real hope—not fake hope. If you're anything like me, you've already had enough taste tests of the fake stuff to know that you don't have time for fake hope. All of the flimsy inspirations and fake hope the world offers can't hold the weight of stress, fatigue, sin, labor pain, or grief. Fake hope can't quell your fears while you sit in the waiting room while your loved one is in surgery. Fake hope can't pick up your broken heart from the floor after you watch a video about abortion. Fake hope can't stay the tide of death that creeps up on us and our loved ones the longer we live on this earth. Fake hope can't look to the past *and* the future, praising Jesus. Fake hope can only make us look back and say things like, "How could I have been such a fool?" As we go through the big story of what God is doing in the world, it will become evident where our fake hopes lie. Be looking for these as you read, and ask the Lord to search your heart. I'm often surprised by the fake hopes I look to for comfort. Would the Lord thrill our hearts as we remember again and again that we need the never-disappointing, real hope of the gospel!

As we taste more and more of the real hope of the gospel, our appetite for fake hope will start to disappear. We need to remember that this kind of growing pain, while painful, is ultimately a *joy*. God creates each of our days with opportunities to be gladhearted, life-giving, glory bearers. Only Christ is strong enough to accomplish this work in and through us. Missional motherhood isn't an exercise in muscling up strength to do stuff for God. Missional motherhood is a walk of faith where the weak (that's *all* of us) must keep before them the scenic view of the cross.

So let's start walking together. We're going to find God's pattern for the missional mothering he has commissioned. And then we're going to hear good news about the Christ who fulfills all of God's promises. Have you heard the saying, "You've got to walk before you fly"? Well, we're going to fly before we walk. In part 1 we're going to fly high and fast over the old, old story. God's pattern will be revealed, and his promises will be given. There are so many threads in God's tapestry of redemptive history, and missional motherhood is only one of them. We're going to be watching the shadow of the cross loom large over the Old Testament. Then, in part 2, we'll walk at a slower pace, pausing to consider some details more closely.

2

Expectations of Our Savior

A Quick Overview of the Old Testament

You may be wondering why there is an overview of the Old Testament in a "mom book." Or you may be wondering why this chapter isn't an overview of *both* the Old and the New Testaments! Both are good questions. Since God is the one who created motherhood, we need to examine his word. For the sake of word count, I've chosen to stick with just the Old Testament narrative in part 1, and I will do a "systematic" approach to the person and work of Jesus Christ in part 2.

When we understand God's big story, we see that missional motherhood is not a *lifestyle*, per se, that is defined by the particular products or things you consume or don't consume or by the activities you do or don't do. A lifestyle is something you can come into or out of according to your culture, preferences, and resources. Redemptive history teaches us that distinctly Christian nurturing is by grace through faith. This is no mere lifestyle; this is resurrection life. We mother others in a way that is consistent with the fact that Easter really happened. So our missional motherhood is not all about what we do or don't put into our bodies or homes, but by living by every word that proceeds from the mouth of God and bearing spiritual fruit that testifies to the reality of the gospel.

To learn about missional motherhood, we start in the Bible—in the beginning—because we know that the Bible is actually God's story. He wrote a book for us.

Our One Need That Trumps Them All

I don't know all the circumstances you will be confronted with today. It would be silly for me to try to address all of the issues that women are facing across the world. But there is one book that does speak to our greatest obstacle, our most daunting hindrance, and our most desperate situation. The Bible tells us who God is and how we can know him.

Our most important need is for a right relationship with God. Every other need you have pales in comparison, like an ant hiding in his dust-bunny house in the basement of a Shanghai skyscraper. Every other need points you to the one, great need of knowing and being known by God. Are you hungry? It's a pointer to help you see that you were designed to live by every word that proceeds from the mouth of God. Are you thirsty? It's a pointer to help you see that your spiritual thirst can be quenched only by the living water Jesus gives. Are you cold? Afraid? Restless? Sad? Lonely? Lost? These needs point you to the one and only God who made you, loves you, and gave his Son to die in your place so you could love him back in spirit and in truth *forever*. Do you feel eternity beating in your heart?

These pictures and pointers serve to remind us of eternal truth. And we need all the reminders we can get! It is astounding to consider all the contrary messages (i.e., lies) that we are faced with each day. This world (Eph. 2:2) is a perverse system architected by Satan. The invisible evil powers and principalities are in league with the Devil, whom Paul called the god of this age (2 Cor. 4:4). These evil powers have designed, organized, and animated the

course of this world in such a way that our fallenness and inclination to sin is only ever validated, endorsed, and encouraged
to truly believe "that's just the way it goes." We catch a whiff of
death and say, "Such is life." We live in a place that is governed
by obscenities that pose as reality, like, "This is all there is," "Just
follow your heart," and "Your best life is now." According to the
world, life is generally meaningless, and humanity is only a group
of optimistic clumps of cells. So a growling stomach simply exists
to remind you that you skipped lunch, and nothing more.

The Bible renews our mind so that we can see through the lies
of this world. This clarity is critical for missional motherhood.
What woman hasn't been lied to about who God is, why he made
the world, and what motherhood means? The course of this world
would have us live as zombies—dead to God and our desperate
need for him.

Praise God that he has not left us to our own devices to plod
along like zombies following the course of this world without in-
terruption. He has intervened. He has revealed himself in his word
and sent his Son, the Word made flesh. In God's word, the Bible,
we read about the real story.

We Need to Ditch the Wrong Story

God is the author of the metanarrative that eats all the mini-
narratives for lunch. To live out God's design for our lives and
follow his plan for our missional motherhood, we need to know
his story.

Women need to know his story for several reasons. First, we
are so easily engrossed in worry over the details of our minuscule
ant stories that we miss the skyscraper. Second, we need to know
his story because stories shape our minds. His word gives us a
distinctly Christian picture of what, how, and why we seek God's
mission in motherhood. Third, when we know and love his story,
it helps prevent us from living out the wrong story. We don't want
to live out the wrong story that is marked by fearful worrying,

never-ending comparing, reluctant mothering, and misguided pur-suing of peace with the world on the world's terms. And, fourth, we need to know the story so we can pass it on to others.

And then there is the reason that engulfs all other reasons: we need to know *Jesus*. Who is he? What is his pattern? How does he fulfill God's promises? What does his pattern and promise fulfill-ing have to do with my mission in mothering?

In the rest of this chapter, we will take a supersonic glide over the Old Testament. Watch the shadow of the cross loom large on the horizon. Let your Spirit-soaked imagination think of all the ways Jesus transforms your motherhood into his mission to nur-ture life. We'll get to implications and applications in part 2, but now is also a good time to dream up some ways that this good news can change the way you mother and disciple. Then, in the rest of this section (part 1), we will zoom a little closer into the story, epoch by epoch. You'll notice some questions in the chap-ters that you may want to examine even further using your Bible study tools.

So go grab a fresh cup of coffee and strap on your seat belt.[4] Your drink may still be warm when you're done reading this quick overview. And hopefully your heart will be warmed too.

Jesus Has Written Us into His Story

His story begins before time began. The triune God—Father, Son, and Holy Spirit—existed in eternity past in perfect fellowship. God created everything you can see (and can't see) for his own glory. The universal kingdom of God was all good.

God created man and woman in his image. God breathed into Adam the breath of life and placed him in a garden. God gave man and woman purpose. God equipped Adam and Eve to subdue the wilderness beyond the garden and expand God's garden-temple over the whole earth. A good and loving Father, God was with and for his children.

But Adam let a crafty serpent twist God's word. Our first

parents rejected God, and instead of living by God's words, they listened to the words of the Serpent, took the forbidden fruit of the knowledge of good and evil, and fell. They sinfully chose to attempt the impossible: independence from God. They attempted to become wise but showed that they were fools. In one bite, death entered the world. Everything on earth went full speed ahead on a course for de-creation. Their hearts turned in on themselves. Like the Serpent, they became liars and accusers. Instead of nurturing, they became self-serving. Instead of testifying to God's purity in the garden he made, their presence polluted it. God pronounced a curse as a result of their sin. There were judgments: thorns, weeds, labor pain, and strife.

But God did not leave his image bearers to suffer his wrath without a way of escape. He promised that the offspring of the woman would defeat the Serpent and his offspring. The cosmic conflict had begun.

Adam believed God's promise by faith. The man and the woman would continue to be coheirs, ambassadors, and image bearers of God. He gave his wife a name that was full of hope, a name full of faith in God's future grace:

> The man called his wife's name Eve, because she was the mother of all living. (Gen. 3:20)

Did you catch that? Death entered creation because of their sin, but new life entered creation because of grace. Eve heaved in labor and gave birth to her son Cain with the help of the Lord. This boy grew up and took the Serpent's side, slaughtering his righteous brother, Abel. We think making the bed only to lie in it again is an exercise in futility. But I wonder what Eve thought of futility at this point? So much for procreation and the promised seed of the woman, right? But the story continues, and hope is never lost as long as God remains faithful to his promises. Eve gave birth to another son, Seth.

We All Need God's Interventions

Even through the multiplied pain of labor, Adam and Eve's off-spring multiplied over the face of the earth. And sin multiplied with them. The hearts of men became so saturated with evil that God sent a deluge to judge mankind and cleanse the earth, but he delivered one family along with some animals. God made a covenant with Noah and reiterated his directive to his image bearers that they were to multiply and rule the earth unto the Lord.

But the flood could not wash clean the heart of man. Noah's offspring multiplied and multiplied in their rebellion. Then God mercifully confused their language at Babel, and the people spread over the face of the earth.

Every kind of nurturing work is an intervention of sorts—stepping between a child and destructive habits, between a friend and her discouragement, between a refugee and homelessness, between a helpless person and neglect. This has been our story since the fall. Not a single one of us has any hope apart from God's gracious intervention. In Genesis 12, we're introduced to the one man God had chosen out of all the people on the earth, a moon-worshiping pagan and his elderly barren wife: Abraham and Sarah.

God made a covenant with Abraham and promised him a spacious homeland, abundant offspring, and worldwide blessing. But how would this elderly couple multiply?

Again, we see God's gracious intervention when Sarah, an old woman, conceived and persevered through labor and gave birth to a son. Sarah was not the only woman who would struggle with the judgment pains that have to do with conception and labor. We're all affected in some way by these things—infertility, miscarriage, and labor—whether this suffering is in our own bodies, or in the body of the woman who bore us, or in the woman who is sitting next to us. Every woman must look to the promised seed of the woman for hope and help.

God overcame the barrenness of many more women after Sarah, showing the strength of his might to provide his promised deliverer.

But Abraham, Isaac, and Jacob lived in tents and did not occupy the land God had promised them or live to see themselves as being a blessing to the whole world. They lived and died by faith.

The end of Genesis is bleak. God's people are living in Egypt, and Abraham's offspring number only about seventy. That might be enough grains of sand for a beach for an ant. God's people had multiplied, but they were wasting away as slaves of a king who was hell-bent on genocide. Mercifully, God raised up midwives who feared him instead of Pharaoh, and they rescued Moses, who would rescue his people when God judged Egypt. The Israelites walked to their freedom through doorways covered in the blood of lambs and through walls lined with seawater.

God's Mission Marches On

On the other side of the water, at a mountain, God gave his children his law. God's global purpose for this people began to take shape. Just like the first man and woman, the children of Israel were called to nurture the whole world, mediating the blessing of God as a kingdom of priests. The people were called to keep the covenant, obey the Lord, depend on him for daily bread, and love him. Clearly, this was a mission the people could not accomplish apart from God's presence.

God dwelt among his people in the tabernacle. In addition to detailed instructions on how to build the tabernacle, God gave his people instructions on how to make sacrifices that were pleasing to him. But God is utterly holy and set apart from sinful man, and the blood of bulls and goats cannot take away sin. So God graciously established a means by which these sacrifices would be tied to a future sacrifice for sin. The people were to live by faith through grace, and to multiply followers of the one, true God. They were to be imagers who would know, obey, and use God's word to spread the knowledge of the Lord over the whole earth. That commission sounds very familiar to us, but we are so easily led astray by lies and idolatry.

Apart from God's intervention, we're no different from faith-less Israel. She was not free from slavery, not really free. Slaves to sin, Israel refused to enter the Promised Land because they'd heard there were giants in the land. Then, when they finally did follow God into the land, they rejected the judges he sent to deliver them. The idols of the nations were more attractive. Those were days of horror when "everyone did what was right in his own eyes" (Judg. 17:6).

Then Israel begged for a king like the pagan nations'. Abraham said that a scepter—a king—would come from Judah. The seed of the woman—the *kingly* line—continued when in the little town of Bethlehem, a descendant of Judah named Boaz took the role of kinsman-redeemer and married a Gentile widow.

Boaz and Ruth's great-grandson, David, was anointed to be king, and he put his trust in the Lord. God established his cov-enant with David, but David sinned. From adultery to murder, this king was obviously flawed. What about his son Solomon? Under Solomon's rule, peace and prosperity multiplied, but so did dozens of wives and a pantheon of idols. Solomon's story makes me won-der if, in our fatigue from caring for others and our weariness from battling our sin, we're happy to settle for a Solomon-like kingdom in our homes. We just want relative peace around the borders of our family, but our hearts are far from the Lord. I know this is my tendency. But praise God—he doesn't let us enjoy peace in this kind of scenario! And he didn't let Israel be content there either.

The kings of Israel rebelled against God ad infinitum. Prophets cried out woes and covenant lawsuits. But the people followed a predictable pattern: conviction of sin, repentance, backsliding, rebellion, repeat. Then the pattern was broken when they were carried out of their homes and into exile. What about the promises of God at that point?

The promises were not repealed; they were still in effect. God's people sang songs about him, his faithfulness, and their longing for him. Along the way, they spoke words expressing what it meant to

live a life of wisdom in "the fear of the LORD" (Prov. 1:7). They
sang a song of songs that hums the melody of an unhindered passion that will one day be consummated as the divine Bridegroom
is joined together with his bride.

Prophets spoke the word of the Lord, saying: "He will be mer-
ciful to us again. You'll be delivered by a new exodus. A new
covenant is coming—not written on stones but on hearts. A new
Sabbath. A new Davidic king. A new temple. God will dwell
among his people again, forever. He will bring us into a new creation where we'll no longer be hindered by sin and death that get
in the way of our enjoyment of God. God will judge his enemies,
and the head of the Serpent will be crushed flat forever under the
foot of his Righteous One."

God did bring a remnant of exiles back to the land. The return,
however, was not a triumphant RESET button. Where was the
new, unprecedented temple? What about the righteous King? What
about God's presence? The people were still entrenched in sin. This
creation didn't look very new. And where was their rest? They were
ruled by a Gentile king who was in charge of helping to spread the
Roman kingdom, not God's kingdom, over the face of the earth.

That reminds me of the common moment when a nurse tells
a laboring mother that she's probably got a long way to go—and
she'll just have to keep waiting and endure patiently, and no, she
doesn't have any guarantees about how much longer it's going to
take. But you can't give up now, because it's too late to go home.
So just try and relax. What?!

Darkness Cannot Overcome the Light

Into this dark situation, a light dawned: "In him was life, and the
life was the light of men" (John 1:4).

Jesus is the one they were waiting for: *the* seed of the woman,
sent not to be served but to serve and to give his life as a ransom
for many; the Son of Man, the Son of God.

But God's enemy did not surrender, saying, "I figured you were coming. All right, here are the captives. Please crush my head now." No. From the moment he was born, Jesus came into conflict with the Enemy of God. The incarnation of the second person of the Trinity was the breaking in of the new creation into the old age that was passing away. The Word of God, who created all things with a word in order to bring about redemption, went about his work undoing the work of sin, Satan, and the course of this world. In his life he suffered rejection and died on the cross at the hands of those who did *not* desire to see his kingdom come and his will be done on earth as it is in heaven.

The events of that weekend two thousand years ago marked the turning of cosmic history. The vindication of the Son's sacrifice—the resurrection of the Christ—is something we must never forget. That bears repeating—you and I must always endeavor to never, ever forget Easter. When it looks like the worry, frustration, fatigue, thanklessness, or futility of your nurturing work is the biggest thing you've got going on right now—remember this! Jesus is alive.

The effects of Jesus's resurrection are not obvious to the naked eye. Our eyes are blinded. That's why the gospel has to be proclaimed—we don't think it up on our own. Dead people don't just wake up and say to themselves,

> I think I need an alien righteousness. Yes! I need a holiness that comes from outside of myself. I bet there's a triune deity who created all things, and the second person of this Trinity became incarnate. I bet the Son of God and Son of Man lived the life I could never live and died as my representative head in order to atone for God's wrath against me. Hmm, I bet if I cling to this God-man by grace through faith, then I will be saved.

No, we can't think this up on our own. We all need to be told the gospel. God is the one who makes us alive, opens our eyes, and invites us to obey his Great Commission, to make disciples of all nations in his power and after his pattern, in view of his promises.

This is the story that I need to remember. This is the story that needs to overrun the minor plot twists in my life: What shall we eat? What shall we drink? What shall we wear? The car is having issues again—what shall we drive? The schedule is too full—what shall we drop? The doctor says there's no hope for healing, just pain management—what shall we change? Your Twitter feed drops a story that makes your heart just explode in your chest—Lord, what shall we do?

I need to know that life is not meaningless, my work is not in vain, and the night is almost over. I need to experience something far bigger than myself—something grand, solid, divine.

There is a forerunner who has taken our flesh up out of the grave into the fullness of resurrected life. Jesus ascended back into heaven (there is a Man in heaven!), and he is worshiped as the slain-yet-conquering Lamb of God. The Father seated him at his right hand, but he's not gone from our lives. His presence is given to his followers through his indwelling Holy Spirit. Through his Spirit he testifies to our hearts that we are children of God. Exile is not the final word, because Jesus ushers in the age of resurrection.

Even now, the promised new creation, which is better than Eden ever could have been, is breaking in through the work of the Spirit in Christ's new humanity of redeemed men, women, and children from every tribe on the face of the earth. The old is gone. The new has come. And the day is coming when the Lamb will return to the earth once more as judge. Every terror and threat in the seen or unseen realm is but a shadow of the wrath of the Lamb against his enemies. With all uncleanness and decrepit evil banished forever, the ones remaining are those who have washed their robes in the atoning blood of the Lamb. Then, at last, his kingdom will come in an unprecedented, fullness-of-age flourish.

God is the one who delivers. Here on earth, we wait with patient endurance for Jesus to return. In the meantime, we have a mission to accomplish by God's grace. It's going to be accomplished both in extraordinary, sweeping revival and in our everyday ministry by the power of the Spirit. We're getting ahead of ourselves now, with all this talk of the end of the age and the beginning of eternity. *Or are we?* We must set our gaze upon the horizon of ever-after with Jesus. We must set our gaze upon the face of God in Christ. We must see and savor Jesus.

Motherhood Is Born

From Creation to Father Abraham

After I submitted a book proposal for *Missional Motherhood*, the thought occurred to me that what I'm attempting to do in part 1 is a fool's errand. How can you possibly summarize something like, oh, you know, *God's epic plan for redemptive history and how motherhood fits in*, in just a few short chapters?

Though I'm confident that this is the right way forward for this book, I still feel intimidated when I try to summarize a story so grand and mind-boggling. I am encouraged, however, that this genre of summary is worthwhile for the busy women who will read this book—because the practice of summary (and the intimidation that goes along with it) is something we do all the time. We all know that intimidated feeling we get when a child asks a profound question. We've all been bewildered when someone we know gets blindsided by tragedy. We all feel frustrated when we realize that precious time is flying by too quickly. We've all sat speechless after reading certain news headlines. The big picture helps us to keep going. To use theater terms, because we are all characters living out a story, we're all ad-libbing according to the script we've subconsciously summarized in our hearts.

What are we actually doing in our motherhood? And to what end is this mission headed? We need to know the big story that starts with the old, old story.

The Story-Writing Word

I said earlier that we were going to watch the shadow of the cross loom large over the Old Testament. The Bible that Jesus read has something to say to us moms today. That idea was new to me when I became a Christian, and I felt as though my brain would either melt in confusion or burst in joy when I heard that the promised seed of the woman in Genesis 3:15 was Jesus. As a new believer, I remember thinking how it was good, *good* news, because all growing up I was under the impression that "the god of the Old Testament" was somehow different from "the god of the New Testament." I thought that the first god was angry with all the sinners, and it's a good thing that that god changed into Jesus and started loving the sinners instead. Boy, was I relieved to discover that I was wrong. Who could possibly trust or love a god who shape-shifts or changes? Praise our triune God—Father, Son, and Holy Spirit—he never changes. He has given us his word, which is one unified message of his plan to glorify himself in saving his lost children.

Reading the Old Testament in the shadow of the cross makes my heart burn within me, like the disciples on the road to Emmaus. The resurrected Christ appeared to them as they were walking along the road, and what he said blew their minds and thrilled their hearts:

> And beginning with Moses and all the Prophets, he interpreted to them in all the Scriptures the things concerning himself. (Luke 24:27)

Can you imagine being there on the road with the disciples when they realized they had been speaking with Jesus, the one who conquered sin and death? The unity of the message of the Bible spreads across all sixty-six books and across both Testaments. When we study this unity, we call it "biblical theology."[5] When Jesus talks about this unity, he shows that the entire Bible is about him.

Of course, there are nuances to interpreting Scripture through this lens; we do not want to find things that are not really there! To put it plainly, your biblical theology is on the right track when you see how all of Scripture points you to the gospel. The Bible is about Jesus Christ and what he did for us in order to restore us to a right relationship with God. Jesus is the central character in God's word. John, a beloved disciple of Jesus, cuts to the chase in the first line in the eyewitness account he wrote:

> In the beginning was the Word, and the Word was with God, and the Word was God. (John 1:1)

Jesus is *the* Word. The Bible is *his* story. He is the Word through whom all things were created.

> For by him all things were created, in heaven and on earth, visible and invisible, whether thrones or dominions or rulers or authorities—all things were created through him and for him. (Col. 1:16)

We need to know how Jesus—his existence, incarnation, teaching, attesting miracles, deeds, death, resurrection, ascension, enthronement, and return—is the governing reality of everything we can see and can't see.

As I said before, it was a relief to find out that the shape-shifting modalism of God is a heresy. It is also a relief to realize and remember that all of life is all about Christ and not about me. If I'm the center of the universe, then I have to fight to keep God, my children, my husband, my friends, my work, and the distracted drivers in the pick-up line at school all orbiting around *me*. Issuing that kind of gravitational pull is exceptionally hard work, and it makes me frustrated (at the very least). All of those planets keep trying to fly off into outer space. When I read that Jesus Christ is the center of everything, I breathe a sigh of relief, repent of my arrogance, and look happily to him in adoring worship. I also have to pick my jaw back up off the floor when I realize that the Word has chosen to create, writing his creation into his story.

God Made Everything You Can See (and Can't See)

It has been said that women are great at multitasking. This may be true, but in my own experience I am not great at keeping in mind the multitude of truths I want to remember. That's why I appreciate basic reminders such as, "In the beginning, God created the heavens and the earth" (Gen. 1:1). It's like a nice, tall glass of perspective when I feel as though the weight of the world is on my shoulders. Before we dismiss this fact of God's creation with a quick "Yes, yes, I know that already," let's pause and consider what it says. Also, before we dismiss this section with a quick "Yes, yes, we covered that in the quick Old Testament overview already," let's pause and remember that we are zooming in now on specific applications of the Old Testament story and how it all applies to our lives.

First, we are creatures. How do we explain all the breathtaking beauty and heartbreaking brokenness we see among us? Human beings—creatures—are both incredible and reprehensible. We are finite, made of dust, given immortal souls that will never die, are painfully addicted to Candy Crush, adorned with innie or outie belly buttons, and are preoccupied with whether the toilet paper is supposed to roll from the top or the bottom. We are Haka-dancing, shawarma-stuffing, love-making, marathon-running, moon-walking, abortion clinic–funding, marriage covenant–vowing, infant-nursing, nuclear bomb–building, orphaned baby bird–rescuing, slave-keeping, slave-freeing, symphony-composing, dolphin-training, motherboard-designing, compassion-giving, refugee-housing, dream-chasing creatures.

Human beings are responsible for discovering honey-cured

bacon and for dropping barrel bombs on Syrian kindergartens. Who do we think we are? Why do we do what we do? To begin to understand ourselves, we need to know that we are *creatures:* accountable, dependent, fragile creatures. We are humble creatures to whom a holy God has revealed himself. The creator God's self-revelation to us is a profound grace that we dare not dismiss or take lightly.

This same creator God, who is before all things, consciously holds us and all things together in himself (Col. 1:17). That is astonishing. The fact that this God would reveal himself to us says so much about who he is. It says that he is the kind of God who would create living beings with a need to know him *and then reveal himself to those creatures so they can know him.* No, God is not needy; we are needy. There is nothing deficient about the triune God in his creation work. His creation is an explosive broadcast of his inherent fullness. The seraphim call out to one another in the throne room of the living God,

> Holy, holy, holy is the LORD of hosts; the whole earth is full of his glory! (Isa. 6:3)

Around the clock, while we are driving to work, crafting a report, feeling a baby kick us from the inside out, sleeping peacefully, or salting the ice on our front porch, the throne room in heaven is reverberating with unceasing praise. Whether we see it or not, we creatures are ever on the receiving end of God's emanating goodness. As children of God, we have been given the privilege of grace that no one could merit. The Westminster Shorter Catechism answers the question "What is the work of creation?" this way:

> The work of creation is God's making all things of nothing, by the word of his power, in the space of six days, and all very good.[6]

Out of nothing, God's powerful word spoke koalas and quasars into existence.

Let us humble ourselves in awe-full, expectant, happy submission to this holy God. God created everything as an overflow of his fullness. Even the heavens declare the glory of God (Psalm 19). And he created you to know him—just think of it! Question: How did God create man? The same catechism explains in sum:

> God created man male and female, after his own image, in knowledge, righteousness and holiness, with dominion over the creatures.[7]

Look for a moment at the unique swirls he imprinted on your thumb. Hold your breath for a second and be conscious of the fact that he made and gives the oxygen that fills your lungs. Why did he create you?

Glorious, Word-Dependent Dust

God spoke into the watery chaos, "Let there be light" (Gen. 1:3). And the light appeared. Then God spoke into the atmosphere, and even more creation appeared: bodies of water, solid earth, plants with seeds for more plants inside, stars, swarming sea creatures, and every beast on the earth that creeps, lumbers, gallops, climbs, or soars. And God saw that it was good.

Then on the sixth day of creation, "God created man in his own image, in the image of God he created him; male and female he created them" (Gen. 1:27).

Genesis 2 gives us a more detailed account of the creation of Adam. "The LORD God formed the man of dust from the ground and breathed into his nostrils the breath of life, and the man became a living creature" (Gen. 2:7). The Creator stooped down to scoop up some earth, personally craft his own *eikon* (Greek "image"), and animate his image bearer with his own breath. The other living creatures were formed out of the ground (Gen. 2:19), but the man, we're told, was the one in whom God breathed his breath of life.

Now, this is curious if we think of God's breath as just oxygen. We breathe oxygen. But so do cheetahs, blue whales, slugs, and parakeets. Did the animals receive God's breath too? No, they just have zoo breath. The word in Hebrew here is *ruah*, which can denote "spirit," "wind," and "breath" (depending on the context). To summarize the majority of the explanations given by biblical scholars, this *ruah* that God breathed into the first man is the same *ruah* that resurrected the lifeless bodies in the valley of dry bones (Ezek. 37:9–10), and the same *ruah* that Jesus breathed on his disciples when he said, "Receive the Holy Spirit" (John 20:22). God's breath alone made Adam "a living soul" (1 Cor. 15:45 NASB).

We are not fully alive unless the Spirit is in us. The creation account shows that it is God who gives life to our souls. But that's not all! He also gives us words for our lives. Have you heard the saying "Words to live by?" Nothing could be closer to the truth about the condition of mankind. God took the man and put him in the garden of Eden, and he gave him words to live by. And then God commanded the man, saying, "You may surely eat of every tree of the garden, but of the tree of the knowledge of good and evil you shall not eat, for in the day that you eat of it you shall surely die" (Gen. 2:16–17). Later, after God created woman, God blessed Adam and Eve and repeated their purpose, "Be fruitful and multiply and fill the earth and subdue it, and have dominion over the fish of the sea and over the birds of the heavens and over every living thing that moves on the earth" (Gen. 1:28). They were two complementary image bearers (male and female), charged with a special task, submitted to God's word, and dependent on God's Spirit.

Look at another familiar passage in one of Paul's letters to Timothy and notice what it says about God's word. Do you see the connection?

All Scripture is breathed out by God and profitable for teaching, for reproof, for correction, and for training in righteousness, that the man of God may be complete, equipped for every good work. (2 Tim. 3:16–17)

We're often tempted to relegate Scripture to a nice tack-on to our lives, but is there any part of life excluded from the passage above? The breath of God turns a man into a living soul. And the breath of God turns God's word into a living work—Scripture— which is wholly sufficient to teach, reprove, correct, train, complete, and equip the man of God for every good work. Every good work! (*Yes*, that means that God means for you to be equipped by his word to do the good work of mothering.) Adam and Eve were given good work to do in expanding God's garden-temple over the face of the earth and multiplying more word-dependent image bearers. And it was God's very word that equipped them to do so. The same is true for us today. As Nehemiah put it, "Both men and women and all who could understand" need God's word (Neh. 8:2, 3).

But we tend to forget this. We often live like it isn't reality. When I wake up in the morning (or am woken up by someone else), many thoughts usually fly into my mind before I think of God's word. I can run through my entire day's agenda, a to-do list or two, and look at pictures of my friends' coffee cups on my phone, all while I'm still lying in bed and before I think of God's word. Do you remember how Jesus rebuked Satan when he tempted him in the wilderness? Jesus quoted Deuteronomy 8:3, saying, "It is written, 'Man shall not live by bread alone, but by every word that comes from the mouth of God'" (Matt. 4:4). God created us wholly dependent upon his word. But how do we do this when words fly at us from every direction, from billboards on the highway, and from the phones by our bedsides? We receive so many mixed messages about our creation, our mission, and our story. Whose words do we choose to live by?

The Crafty Snake

Living by every word that comes from the mouth of God was Adam and Eve's privileged task and ontology, or *reality*. God speaks, and mankind lives, by whatever it is that God has said.

That's reality. But you don't have to read too far into Genesis until you are introduced to the message Confuser—God's Enemy. Satan wanted the story to be about him instead:

> You said in your heart,
>   "I will ascend to heaven;
> above the stars of God
>   I will set my throne on high;
> I will sit on the mount of assembly
>   in the far reaches of the north;
> I will ascend above the heights of the clouds;
>   I will make myself like the Most High." (Isa. 14:13–14)

The utter arrogance of those "I will" statements makes me shudder. God created man and woman to be his image bearers and his managers over creation, so he gave them his words to live by. They needed God's words, and God's story, to guide their lives. But the Enemy schemed a way to make the story about him. Satan tricked the man and the woman to bear his decrepit image, spread his kingdom of hell, and live by his poisonous words instead.

Satan entered the Serpent, and Adam allowed him into God's pristine garden, where no unholy thing dwelled. Adam allowed the Serpent to speak to Eve, his glorious coheir and vice-regent over all creation, and Satan hissed inklings of doubt into the woman's ears,

> Did God actually say, "You shall not eat of any tree in the garden"? (Gen. 3:1)

The first hiss of doubt tricked the woman's soul. Perhaps God's words cannot be trusted. Perhaps there is a better word than God's. Perhaps we should be the judge of God.

In Eve's reply, we hear the arrogance of a legalist. She minimized the freedom God had given them to freely eat and answered the Serpent, "We may eat of the fruit of the trees in the garden" (Gen. 3:2). Next, she made up her own rule about not *touching* the fruit, and then she minimized God's judgment from "You shall *surely* die," to "*Lest* you die" (Gen. 3:3). Satan affirmed Eve's doubts by saying, "You will not surely die. For God knows that when you eat of it your eyes will be opened, and you will be like God, knowing good and evil" (Gen. 3:4–5). Meanwhile, Adam stood by, listening to God's word being questioned, judged, twisted, and misapplied. He ought to have subdued the satanic Serpent and stepped on that snake's head right then and there. Adam and Eve were already like God, and they trusted God to tell them what they needed to know. Who did this liar think he was, repudiating God and making his own counterpromises? This is a thread that runs throughout human history—the Serpent's lies. There are many parts in part 2 where we will examine that thread a little more closely and see how it affects the way we mother and disciple others. For now, let's keep tracking with the big story.

We know how the rest of the story goes. Adam and Eve rejected God's word and rebelled against his rule. How did God respond? God called out to his exposed, fallen children as they hid from him in the bushes.

The Promised Seed of Woman

"Where are you?" God called to the man (Gen. 3:9). Can you hear God's heartbeat of mercy in this question? It's the same question we all needed to come to grips with when we were saved. *Where are you?* The implication, of course, when God asks this question, is that we are not with him. And the mercy in it implies a second question: *Do you know you're not with me?* There was a time in my life when I didn't know I was not with the Lord. I believed that I was "covered" because of my familiarity with the church and Christianity. After all, God and I weren't at odds with each other, or so I thought. But such coverings are mere fig leaves in the eyes of God. By the grace of God alone, when I heard that question,

"Where are you?" in my heart, I didn't retreat further back into the bushes of pride and shame to hide from God but ran out to him so I could be clothed in Christ. And so God called to Adam. In an act of mercy, he did not let Adam and Eve hide from him. God initiates.

We can read the dialogue between God and the man and the woman in Genesis 3:9–13. Their guilt is exposed in plain language, but instead of repenting before God, they blamed their rebellion on their circumstances. Adam blamed Eve, and Eve blamed the Serpent. And so began the human legacy of avoiding the confession of our sin in a futile attempt to avoid the God who is everywhere and sees all things. At this point in our recounting of the big story, it may be good to take a moment to pause, acknowledge our own propensity to rack up points in the blame game, and admit to God that we need his grace.

And we don't stop there. We recall what happened next. God had mercy on us. Even in the pronouncement of his just judgments, we can hear God's heartbeat of mercy. The Lord God cursed the Serpent and revealed his master plan to redeem his fallen children. Listen to this good news:

> I will put enmity between you and the woman, and between your offspring and her offspring; he shall bruise your head, and you shall bruise his heel. (Gen. 3:15)

Did you hear the hope? You are reading this book because the Lord God did not immediately extinguish the man and the woman (as he rightly could have done). Whatever condition our lives are in today, blood rushes through our veins and our lungs fill with air because God is showing us mercy. There are many seasons in a woman's life, as we will see, but for now, understand that you are in a season of life. And if you are in Christ, you are in an eternal season of everlasting life. The mercy God showed the man and the woman was for a purpose—that he might accomplish his plan through the offspring of the woman.

The Mother of All Living

At this point in the book, your mind may be swimming with questions about Eve, her multiplied pain in childbearing, her "desire" for her husband (Gen. 3:16), and every related question under the sun. For the sake of brevity we cannot head into these deep waters in this chapter, but later we will wade into some of these issues. But now (as always, and especially as we are introduced to this part of his story), is a time for worshipful gratitude. We receive God's word with thankfulness because we know we are utterly needy. We submit to him with glad hearts because he has not given us what we deserve. Our past is all grace. Our future is all grace. And *whatever* circumstances you find yourself in today—it's all grace. The eyes of every mother must turn to her God, who has given her the gift of nurturing life in the face of death.

Adam believed God's promise of future grace, and in an act of faith he gave his wife a name that suited her. It was a name that was pregnant with hope:

> The man called his wife's name Eve, because she was the mother of all living. (Gen. 3:20)

Through her, the woman, the promised Serpent crusher would come. "And the LORD God made for Adam and for his wife garments of skins and clothed them" (Gen. 3:21). So God restored Adam and Eve to himself through slaughtering an innocent and covering up their shame. All this he did of his own initiative. Do you see how he established the pattern for our salvation?

The Cleansing Flood

In Genesis 4:1 we read that "Adam knew Eve his wife, and she conceived and bore Cain." The mother of all living heaved in multiplied labor pains and gave birth to a son. Then she said, "I have gotten a man with the help of the LORD." Would this baby boy grow up to crush the head of the Serpent? The answer, we know, had to be no, for Cain was of Adam's seed, born fallen. In time, Cain allied with the destroyer of life, and he murdered his righteous brother, Abel.

In the face of death, however, life continued. People multiplied over the face of the earth. And their sin multiplied along with them. Generation after perverse generation, the distorted image bearers swarmed over the earth, ruling and subduing *not* in the name of the Lord. "The LORD saw that the wickedness of man was great in the earth, and that every intention of the thoughts of his heart was only evil continually" (Gen. 6:5). But there was one man who found favor in the eyes of the Lord—Noah (Gen. 6:8). Through no righteousness of his own, but only through God's mercy, Noah (along with his family) was saved from the wrath of God. God sent a deluge to cleanse the earth of evil and wipe out all of mankind (minus one family). Noah's ark was a floating zoo of hope, containing the future of humanity and borne along by God's promise to send the Messiah.

After the flood, and with their sea legs still adjusting to dry land, God made a covenant with Noah and repeated the command he had originally given to Adam: "Be fruitful and multiply and fill the earth" (Gen. 9:1). But the floodwater could not wash clean the hearts of the men and women inside the ark. Noah's sons and their wives gave birth to children who were also fallen, just as they were. Rebellious image bearers began to fill the earth once more. What hope did the life-giving nurturers have then? Where was the promised Serpent-crushing Messiah? The witness to this hope was lost, and the people set themselves to work on a tower for the sole purpose of exalting themselves above the heavens. "Come, let us build ourselves a city and a tower with its top in the heavens, and let us make a name for ourselves, lest we be dispersed over the face of the whole earth" (Gen. 11:4). God came down and mercifully confused their language so that they couldn't understand each other, and they abandoned their foolish quest (for the time being). Incidentally, where would we be without God's interventions in our lives? Our only hope is that God would overcome us with his mercy. The dragon thrashes for the promised seed of the woman, attempting to snuff out the hoped-for son. And the nations will rage until that Serpent and his offspring are subdued forever.

Barrenness Is No Obstacle

So far in the story, the fruit of the womb had not produced final deliverance, by any stretch of the maternity wear. But the triumph of life through multiplied labor pain prevailed! Life in the face of death continued, which was abundant evidence of the patience and promise of a holy God. We, like the matriarchs of our faith, have our hands full with the abundant evidence of God's patience toward us. We do not have enough hours in the day to accomplish all the nurturing work he has given us. Whether we have zero biological children or twelve, our opportunities to nurture others and "mother" others in the faith are overwhelming.

God revealed himself to an elderly couple of moon-worshiping pagans named Abraham and Sarah. He told them that he was writing them into his story:

> Go from your country and your kindred and your father's house to the land that I will show you. And I will make of you a great nation, and I will bless you and make your name great, so that you will be a blessing. I will bless those who bless you, and him who dishonors you I will curse, and in you all the families of the earth shall be blessed. (Gen. 12:1–3)

Isn't this story marvelous? The Lord chose an elderly couple, who had exactly zero children, in order to show the world just how committed he was to keeping his promise.

Global blessing is not a new idea here, because we remember the creation mandate—to subdue the earth as God's vice-regents in order to spread his kingdom. God's mission is still on; his people are still commissioned. Now, God has made his covenant with Abraham, promising to be his shield and give him a great reward (Gen. 15:1–21). But, as Captain Obvious Abraham pointed out, he and his wife still had no children. An infertile womb was not a wrench in God's plan, but a vessel to show his glory. God overcame Sarah's barrenness, and she gave birth to a son, whom she named Isaac. She named him "laughter," which probably reminded the old woman of her bright hope as she cradled her newborn. The theme of barrenness is traced all over God's story as he brings together men with infertile women in this family of faith. God's power is made evident in our human weakness so that he is the one who gets the glory. It is his story.

This is your heritage, whether you have zero biological children or so many that the people around you are always asking, "Did you mean to have that many kids?" It's your heritage because it is a heritage *of faith* in the God who overcomes our spiritual barrenness and raises the dead. The hope of these ancients is the same as our hope. We do not put our hope in what is born of perishable seed (1 Pet. 1:23)—"the will of the flesh nor of the will of man" (John 1:13). We put our hope in the imperishable gospel.

Our pace is quickening as we fly over redemptive history. As we continue to soar over the Old Testament, we'll keep watching the horizon for the promised seed of the woman. Next, we pick up God's story with Jacob's children in Egypt.

4

The God Who Delivers

From Egypt to the Promised Land

God made granite mountains rise up out of the seas. He gave kangaroos peculiar pockets to carry their joeys as they hop on their enormous Hobbit feet. He designed every ice crystal that floats down from the clouds to your child's snowflake-tasting tongue. We know, from looking at creation, that our ability is not worth comparing to the Lord's. But instead of looking to God for the deliverance we need, we keep reaching down for our own bootstraps to try to pull ourselves up.

We subdue the earth and invent new technologies for the sake of making a name for ourselves. We give birth to children, glory only in the fact that they bear our image—his eyes and her hair color—and we fail to thank God for his help. Across cultures, from nomadic Bedouin to suburban hipsters, we try to embody the images of created things and grasp for the promises they cannot deliver. Is there hope for such fallen people? Who will stand as a mediator between sinful people who can barely focus a single thought on their holy Creator?

We are teachers of one another. Pastors, women's ministry leaders, fathers, and mothers. Is it possible that lost men, women, and children might be restored to a saving relationship with God through the witness of already-restored image bearers?

The Failed Mission to Worship

Out of all the wicked people on earth, God actually chose to save some. In Genesis 12, we meet Abraham and Sarah, elected by God to serve his mission to glorify himself in all creation. Shadows of Christ and his cross were all over this couple and their family: Abraham's near-sacrifice of his only son on the mountain and God's provision of the sacrifice; the faithful servant's quest to search out a bride for a father's son; a blessing and inheritance obtained by hiding in the covering of another; what envious brothers meant for evil, God meant for good in the saving of many lives. But still, the patriarchs lived in a foreign land. They didn't live in the land God promised them; neither did they live to see themselves as issuing forth blessings for all the nations. All these people lived—and died—by faith.

So now, even though they've multiplied in number a little bit, their experience of God's promises is nowhere near completely fulfilled. At the end of the book of Genesis, their number is about seventy people. The book of Exodus picks up God's story, where we read that "the people of Israel were *fruitful* and *increased* greatly; they *multiplied* and grew exceedingly strong, so that the land was *filled* with them" (Ex. 1:7). But then we read that they'd multiplied into a great host of slaves. The Israelites were not only *not* living in their promised land, but they were being subjected to cruel treatment and infanticide. So, God raised up midwives who nurtured life in the face of death and rescued many baby boys from death at the behest of a paranoid Pharaoh. Instead of sacrificing the helpless babies, they put their own lives on the line. "So God dealt well with the midwives. *And the people multiplied and grew very strong*" (Ex. 1:20). An Egyptian princess drew him up out of the water, and Moses later drew the people up out of Egypt through the Red Sea.

You know the story. God revealed himself to Moses at the burning bush and shared his name, "I AM" (Ex. 3:14). He commissioned Moses to go to the Pharaoh and speak for him, saying, "Israel is my firstborn son, and I say to you, 'Let my son go that he may serve me.' If you refuse to let him go, behold, I will kill your firstborn son" (Ex. 4:22–23). Pharaoh refused; his heart hardened; and then came the bloody river, frogs, lice, hail, and other sundry plagues that fell upon the Egyptians. He did not heed the warning, and he refused to let God's firstborn son, Israel, go. Finally, God sent forth his avenging angel to kill all of the Egyptians' firstborn children, including Pharaoh's firstborn son, just like he had said.

The Hebrews escaped this judgment by following God's instructions to a tee. He told them to kill a Passover lamb and hide behind its blood, which they were to paint over their doorways. God's wrath passed over them, and their lives were spared. The rebellious Pharaoh relented, let Israel go, but then chased them through the desert to the Red Sea. Israel was stuck between an army and a huge body of water. But God miraculously parted the water for them, and God's people walked to freedom through doorways of blood and walls of water. And the people sang! This was no end-zone peacock strut on the other side of the Red Sea. This was a worshipful reveling in the covenant love of the Lord—their deliverer. God's people began to see that it was only by supernatural deliverance that they would be brought into the land that was promised to them. Impress this event on your mind and heart, keep careful watch in the story for reminders of this magnificent rescue, and understand that it is a type of other deliverances to come.

Abort Mission?

It looked like everything sad was coming untrue for the Hebrews. Their backs, bent over from generations of slave labor, began to straighten. They were on their way to the land God had promised them—at last! But their hearts were still turned in on themselves. Time and again, while they trekked across the desert, following Moses, the leader whom God appointed, they grumbled against God and quarreled with Moses. You may find yourself shaking your head as you read through half of Exodus. What happened in a wilderness far, far away (well, not *that* far from where I'm writing right now) seems to us like an obscure historical incident. Regardless of where you are living, this scene is so close to home that it's not funny. God feeds us with our own bread from heaven and water from rocks, but we're not happy unless we have whatever it is *they* have over there in Egypt. A quick skim through pictures of other people's lunches on social media tells me that I'm not so different from the Israelite women who were grumpy about the manna they baked into bread. The hearts of the Hebrews and our hearts today need renewal.

You have probably heard the saying, "God does not have a 'Plan B.'" It sounds trite and truncated, but it is true. What happened at Sinai is a colorful illustration of God's deliberate, unfailing plan to fill the earth with his glory as he accomplishes that mission through his people. Moses went up the mountain to meet with God. And would you believe what God said?

> Thus you shall say to the house of Jacob, and tell the people of Israel: "You yourselves have seen what I did to the Egyptians, and how I bore you on eagles' wings and brought you to myself. Now therefore, if you will indeed obey my voice and keep my covenant, you shall be my treasured possession among all peoples, for all the earth is mine; and you shall be to me a kingdom of priests and a holy nation. These are the words that you shall speak to the people of Israel." (Ex. 19:3–6)

Wow. God would commit himself to a bunch of grouchy-pants complainers and turn them into a kingdom of commissioned priests. But when the people heard the thunder and the trumpet and saw the smoke and the clouds, they shrank back from letting

God speak to them (Ex. 20:18–21). The people were to remain at the foot of the mountain, the priests and seventy elders went a little bit up the mountain, and Moses alone went up Mount Sinai to meet with God and receive God's good law for the people. Then "Moses came and told the people all the words of the Lord and all the rules. And all the people answered with one voice and said, 'All the words that the Lord has spoken we will do'" (Ex. 24:3). Moses performed a blood ceremony with the blood of sacrificed animals and said, "Behold the blood of the covenant that the Lord has made with you in accordance with all these words" (Ex. 24:8). And there you have it—a covenant between Yahweh and his people.

For the next forty days and forty nights, Moses was in the midst of the swirling smoke and consuming fire of Sinai, as God wrote down his commandments on tablets of stone for the people's instruction. On that mountain, Yahweh revealed to Moses the things he had planned to use in order to facilitate his relationship to his people. He is I AM, the holy one of Israel. He gave Moses instructions for his tabernacle and the ar . . . Wait. What? His tabernacle? *A dwelling place for God among men?* Yes, that's right. This good news must have shocked the people to their core:

> There I will meet with the people of Israel, and it shall be sanctified by my glory. . . . I will dwell among the people of Israel and will be their God. And they shall know that I am the Lord their God, who brought them out of the land of Egypt that I might dwell among them. I am the Lord their God. (Ex. 29:43, 45–46)

The tabernacle facilitated God's presence among his people. We who have the indwelling Spirit now should sober our hearts in wonder at this. How often we forget. How presumptuous we often are. "God is with you!" we quip, and indeed God is with us. But his presence among us came at a price that none of us could have paid.

So back to the Israelites. How was this plan going to work?

How would a holy God dwell among a sinful people? We continue with the instructions Yahweh gave to Moses on the mountain. These instructions would be shadowy copies of heavenly things. In essence, their observance of his instructions regarding sacrifices would be tied by faith to a future, ultimate sacrifice for their sins. He gave them instructions for the ark of the covenant, the table for the bread of the Presence, the golden lampstand, the bronze altar, the courtyard, the oil lamp, the priestly garments, the consecration of his priests, the altar of incense, the bronze basin for priestly washing, and the Sabbath day. "And he gave to Moses, when he had finished speaking with him on Mount Sinai, the two tablets of the testimony, tablets of stone, written with the finger of God" (Ex. 31:18).

God gave words to his needy, Word-dependent creatures. These words, the law, would serve as a guardian until Christ came (Gal. 3:23–24). These sacrifices were tied to a future, ultimate sacrifice for their sins. These patterns and promises were the means by which he would dwell among his people. "For when Moses was about to erect the tent, he was instructed by God, saying, 'See that you make everything according to the pattern that was shown you on the mountain'" (Heb. 8:5). God gave gifts of grace to give to his people so he could give them himself. What more could anyone *ever* need? Well, besides, of course, *the real thing* to which these shadowy things pointed! One day the Lord their God raised up from among them a prophet like Moses; they listened to him (Deut. 18:15; see also Acts 3:22; 7:37). And then in the fullness of time, Jesus their final Prophet came. And he uttered the words, "Do not think that I have come to abolish the Law or the Prophets; I have not come to abolish them but to fulfill them" (Matt. 5:17).

Reboot Mission

But we're getting ahead of ourselves. You would think that Israel would have been eager to get ahead with God's instructions. After all, God had rescued them from slavery and was going to deliver them to the land he promised. They were pumped up and ready to follow Yahweh wherever he would lead. Right?

Well, it didn't exactly happen like that at Sinai base camp. While Moses was on the mountain, his brother Aaron (their priest) listened to the people and busied himself with organizing an idolatrous orgy centered around a golden calf. What in the world? Clearly, God's people did not see their mission clearly. They did not see that they were saved to worship God. They did not have in mind God's commission to them—to fill the earth with worshipers who loved the glory of God.

Was all lost? Not if you have faith in the God who keeps his promises. Moses demonstrated his persistent (and almost presumptuous) faith in God's faithfulness:

> Remember Abraham, Isaac, and Israel, your servants, to whom you swore by your own self, and said to them, "I will multiply your offspring as the stars of heaven, and all this land that I have promised I will give to your offspring, and they shall inherit it forever." (Ex. 32:13)

Would you have the confidence to ask God to remember his vow? Moses was a bold brother. But his boldness before God was predicated on what God had said about himself. God will absolutely keep his covenant, and he will wholly uphold his holiness. He will crush the head of his Enemy, Satan. He will preserve his holy nation of image-bearing priests to mediate his blessing to the whole world. He will be glorified among all the nations of the earth as surely as the waters cover the sea. God is faithful. Do not presume, dear life nurturers, that you are ever alone in the good work this God has commissioned you to do.

The Dwelling Place of God among Men

The word *tabernacle* means tent. And although it was a temporary tent, it was neither a typical Hebrew home nor a gigantic pop-up camper. Although the Hebrews put it together according to God's instructions, the tabernacle was a symbolic shadow of a heavenly reality that is outside the bounds of human engineering and technology. You might even think of it like you would a window—peering through the lampstand, bread, curtains, oil, and blood—to Christ. The tabernacle was given to aid our spiritual vision, though no detail was left to our imagination. The Lord God made it clear that there would be no ad-libbing when it came to his dwelling place and the rules concerning how sinful people could approach his holy presence (Ex. 25:40). And neither should we ad-lib our own reconciliation to God. We're completely dependent on God's revelation to us in the way we relate to him.

He provided for his people then, and he provides for his people now. Oh, how he provides for us as we nurture life and make disciples. If we took a time-out right now to write down *all* the ways God provides for us to have fellowship with him and with those around us, we wouldn't have any time to get through the rest of the big story! Let's press in and look through the window of the tabernacle a little closer to see the specific ways God provided for Israel.

If we went camping (an activity that I personally prefer to avoid), then we would have some liberty in terms of how we set up camp. Shall we build a fire pit out in the clearing, or just use the barbecue that's already there? Shall we string a line to hang up our food away from the varmints, or just leave the food in the car? These are all questions that I would be happy to never have to consider. And these are the kinds of questions the Israelites were not given liberty to innovate when it came to the tabernacle. The layout, furniture, and sacrifices of God's tabernacle were provided strictly according to his specifications. Otherwise, they would not have represented the reality of the heavenly things (Heb. 9:11–24). God's specific design is crucial in understanding God's specific purpose for the wilderness tabernacle.

First, think of the boundaries of the tabernacle. Remember

how the mountain trembled in smoke, fire, thunder, and lightning? The congregation was allowed to remain at the foot of Sinai, the priests went a little way up the mountain, and only Moses was permitted to go to the top of the mountain into the presence of God. The tabernacle had boundaries that corresponded to Sinai. And further, as G. K. Beale points out and expounds upon in his book *The Temple and the Church's Mission*, the tabernacle (and later, the temple) corresponds to the boundaries of the universe.[8]

Before your mind melts with joy, let your Scripture-soaked imagination hang on to this quick thought: the outer court of the tabernacle where priests made sacrifices corresponds to the world in which we live. We Christians are to present our bodies as a living sacrifice (holy and acceptable) in this place, which is our spiritual worship (Rom. 12:1–2). Jesus our High Priest entered in to the Most Holy Place in heaven, the throne room of the Most High God, bringing his blood as the sacrifice for the new covenant. We'll talk about this much more in due time, but for now, fellow nurturers, know this: when we serve others—discipling, changing diapers, saving lives at a pregnancy resource center, stacking chairs after Sunday school—it is more than human do-goodery. It is holy and acceptable worship done unto the Lord. All of it is possible because our High Priest, Jesus, went before us. His blood speaks for us in our atonement and in our priestly work done here in the outer court of the world. Your service unto God is *holy*.

God had not walked among his people since the garden (Gen. 3:8). But then, through the ministry of the priestly work done in this tabernacle, God chose to make his dwelling place among his people again:

> I will make my dwelling among you, and my soul shall not abhor you. And I will walk among you and will be your God, and you shall be my people. (Lev. 26:11–12)

Over the high fence of the tabernacle, the congregation could see the massive pillar of smoke of the presence of God when it descended over the Most Holy Place. God is holy, and he cannot abide in the presence of sinners. Atonement must be made, so he initiated a way for the worshiper to enter his presence by proxy. A priest would bring the appropriate and acceptable sacrifice in to the altar. Only after being cleansed in the basin designated for priestly washing could the representative offer sacrifices inside the tent for the people outside. "For I am the LORD your God. Consecrate yourselves therefore, and be holy, for I am holy" (Lev. 11:44). God gave his word-dependent creatures his holy word, written by his own hand on tablets of stone. He spoke to them of atonement for their sins and gave them a window through which they could look to see something better than an annual Day of Atonement (Lev. 16:30). Can you see Jesus through the tabernacle window?

> He has no need, like those high priests, to offer sacrifices daily, first for his own sins and then for those of the people, since he did this once for all when he offered up himself. (Heb. 7:27)

> He entered once for all into the holy places, not by means of the blood of goats and calves but by means of his own blood, thus securing an eternal redemption. (Heb. 9:12)

> But as it is, he has appeared once for all at the end of the ages to put away sin by the sacrifice of himself. (Heb. 9:26)

> For since the law has but a shadow of the good things to come instead of the true form of these realities, it can never, by the same sacrifices that are continually offered every year, make perfect those who draw near. (Heb. 10:1)

The details of the tabernacle worship highlight the manifold perfections of the person and work of Jesus. Someday a perfect High Priest would come and put an end to the sacrifices, once and for all, by sacrificing himself.

Arise, O Lord

And so God, their God, chose to go before them and take them in to the land he had promised to their forefathers. In the wilderness, time and again, the people learned that one does not want to go where God is not, and one does not want to leave the place where God dwells. The nearness of God was their good. The presence of God is the people's good. Hundreds of years later, the psalmist Asaph put it this way in Psalm 73:

> For behold, those who are far from you shall perish;
>> you put an end to everyone who is unfaithful to you.
> But for me it is good to be near God;
>> I have made the Lord GOD my refuge,
>> that I may tell of all your works. (Ps. 73:27–28)

Did you notice the assumption in that psalm? For some people (God's enemies), the nearness of God is not their good. When the cloud went before the people and the priests took up the ark to follow, Moses said: "Arise, O LORD, and let your enemies be scattered, and let those who hate you flee before you." And when the ark rested, Moses said: "Return, O LORD, to the ten thousand thousands of Israel" (Num. 10:35–36). The pattern was established: the people had no business going anywhere if they were not following their God. And in rescue after rescue, provision after miraculous provision, the people saw that when they were apart from God, they were helpless.

Doesn't this history sound familiar to you? It does to me. And when I say "history," I mean earlier this morning when I worried, "What shall we eat? What shall we drink? What shall we wear?" and I forgot that life is more than food and clothing. Our ability to provide for the people who are in our care does not come from *our* ability at all, as though we are anything. But our supply—energy, time, resources (coffee!)—comes from the Lord. We have no business going anywhere that God doesn't lead us. We have nothing in ourselves to give. We, like the children of Israel, are utterly dependent on God, whether or not we recognize or appreciate it. If you think you have a hard time remembering this, you'll see in a moment that you're not alone in that struggle.

The warrior God went before his people as their leader. He demonstrated time and again that he was faithful to his mission to exalt his name in all the earth. And the extraordinary, grace-laden means by which he would do this, this exalting of his name, would be in the way he chose to love his people and bless them for no other reason than that he had decided to do so. Yahweh is a covenant-keeping God. Blessings abound in his presence—kingdom blessings. Forgetful Israel needed to be reminded of this, as do we. Consider the blessing that God instructed Moses to have Aaron, the priest, speak over the people:

> The LORD bless you and keep you;
> the LORD make his face to shine upon you and be gracious
>   to you;
> the LORD lift up his countenance upon you and give you
>   peace. (Num. 6:24–26)

Those words are repeated in the liturgy of some Christian worship gatherings, and it's easy to miss their significance for familiarity. It's good to pause and think about what God is really saying. God said that this blessing indicated that his name would be upon the people of Israel, and that he would bless them (Num. 6:27). Promise-keeping Yahweh will exalt his name in all the earth, the nations will see and fear him, and all the earth will be filled with his glory. This peace he speaks of is more than a tranquil summer afternoon on the patio with a lemonade. It's the peace that surpasses understanding over and against any kind of peace that the world gives. It's the peace of God, which is given to us by Christ. Listen to what the ultimate Passover Lamb said at the Last Supper:

> Peace I leave with you; my peace I give to you. Not as the world gives do I give to you. Let not your hearts be troubled, neither let them be afraid. (John 14:27)

Don't let our hearts be troubled? Hours after he spoke those words, Jesus was lifted up on the cross. His Father poured out every last drop of his wrath on his innocent Son as he hung on the tree. Three days later, his grave was empty. Forty days later, he ascended back to heaven. The Lord's countenance was literally "lifted up" as he ascended, and a cloud took him out of the disciples' sight. Jesus gave them his perfect peace and his promised Holy Spirit. He gave them his name to spread the good news of his coming and promised return.

Centuries before, in the wilderness, the host of people were not so sure that this blessing was coming and the promise was true. Only in hindsight would people such as King David look back and say things like this:

> O God, when you went out before your people,
>> when you marched through the wilderness,
> the earth quaked, the heavens poured down rain,
>> before God, the One of Sinai,
>> before God, the God of Israel. (Ps. 68:7–8)

God is clearly the one on a mission here. And he will not fail. Moses sent twelve spies into the Promised Land, which was flowing with milk and honey, and only two spies came back with confidence in Yahweh. The other ten men saw the giants in the land and quaked in their sandals. They were not so sure that the Lord could do what he said he would do. Perhaps, they thought, the promises of God were not theirs for the taking.

How Long?

Rampant, faithless doubt spread throughout the camp. Like the Israelites, we often want to ask that question of the Lord, "How long?" But when God responded to the doubts of that faithless generation, he posed a similar question in a way that gives us pause as well:

> How long will this people despise me? And how long will they not believe in me, in spite of all the signs that I have done among them? (Num. 14:11)

God judged that generation, and they wandered for the rest of their lives. Joshua and Caleb were spared in order to lead their children into the Promised Land. But the people still didn't get it. Against Moses and against God's pronouncement of judgment, they tried to get in to the land. "But they presumed to go up to the heights of the hill country, although neither the ark of the covenant of the LORD nor Moses departed out of the camp" (Num. 14:44). They were soundly defeated by the locals. But God knew their weakness and had compassion on his people. He gave them more reminders to follow his word and more warnings "not to follow after your own heart and your own eyes, which you are inclined to whore after" (Num. 15:39). He reminded them that he is the God who brought them up out of the land of Egypt. He reminded them that he is still "the LORD your God" (Num. 15:41).

How long would it be until the children of Israel were faithful to their part of the covenant? Not ever. An unparalleled intervention would have to occur. Someone would have to keep the covenant on their behalf. Many years later, a teacher of the law, Nicodemus, came to Jesus in the night to ask him questions. As a law follower, he was burdened by this "how long" question. Nicodemus wanted to know how it was that Jesus was doing the incredible things he was doing—his miracles and his authoritative teaching concerning the law. After Jesus described the new birth as a new creation life that must occur if one wants to see the kingdom, he retold a story from this wilderness time in Israel's history. In Numbers 21, the people were doing that restless grumbling bit and spoke out against God yet again:

Why have you brought us up out of Egypt to die in the wilderness? For there is no food and no water, and we loathe this
worthless food. (Num. 21:5)

That "worthless food," to be precise, was the miraculous manna
from heaven that God rained down on them to feed them in their
wanderings. In response to their treachery, God sent fiery snakes
among the people to bite and kill them. The snake-scared people
confessed their sin and cried out to the Lord in repentance. So
God told Moses to make a snake and put it on a pole so the
people could look at it and live (Num. 21:5–9). Jesus explained
to Nicodemus that another lifting up was going to take place, but
this time the result would bring forth new creation life: "And as
Moses lifted up the serpent in the wilderness, so must the Son of
Man be lifted up, that whoever believes in him may have eternal
life" (John 3:14–15).

God rains down his blessings on us, and his mercy transforms
the way we mother others. But sometimes it's easy to think that we
are the ones offering the mercy to those whom we serve. There is
a clear implication for us as mothers in this: Do *you* want mercy?
Look to Christ in faith. This is the mercy that your loved ones
need most, as well. Are there children in your care, disciples in
your church, neighbors in your apartment building? Point them
to the cross. All who believe in Jesus will be rescued from something more deadly than venomous snakes. They will be rescued
from the wrath of God. No provision God gives you could ever
be worthless. He ransoms us with the precious blood of Christ,
the spotless Lamb of God, from the futile ways we inherited from
our forefathers (1 Pet. 1:18–19). If you have raised or are rais-
ing children, you may sometimes look to your husband and ask,
"Will these kids ever learn?" It's about this point in our reading
of the Old Testament when we start to ask the very same about
the children of Israel. These people keep walking in the futile ways
inherited from their forefathers. As we read on, we ask with a

gnawing sense of dread in our hearts: Will they ever learn to look to God's provision?

Circumcised Hearts

Well, the babies who were born in the wilderness grew up. Forty years before, their parents had walked through the Red Sea on dry land. Then, in the shadow of Mount Nebo, the people camped out in the flatlands of Moab. Through Moses, God restated his covenant with Israel on the doorstep of the Promised Land. Joshua and Caleb stood ready to lead the people in because Moses was told to stay out. His disobedience at the rock in the wilderness of Zin had disqualified him from entering the land (Num. 20:12; 27:14). Moses's disobedience and the consequences for his sin are perplexing at first glance. Sure, he didn't do what God said that time, but was it that important? It was and is. Would *this* next generation prove to be faithful in areas where Moses had not? It's hard to overstate how important it is to remember who this God is whom we serve. *He is holy.* Though we might imagine what God will do with our everyday mothering ministry, God is the one who tests our hearts (1 Thess. 2:4). Missionary and speaker Elisabeth Elliot said in her testimony at Urbana, "Obedience is our task. The results of that obedience are God's and God's alone."[9] And so we make glad-hearted, faithful stewardship our aim in all our nurturing work.

In Deuteronomy, a short national history is rehearsed. Who is the chief actor? It is Yahweh, who is ever faithful. Oh, the mighty deeds he has done on behalf of his people! To uphold his name among the nations and spread his glory in every land, he loved his people, despite their rebellion. Despite their complaining, faithless grumbling, and fearful skittishness to believe him, Yahweh chose Israel to be "a people for his treasured possession, out of all the peoples who are on the face of the earth" (Deut. 7:6). His sovereign love was set on them, and he brought them into a land beyond their wildest dreams (Deut. 8:7–10). Could this be theirs for the having? Did the people whose parents had a shoddy track record of keeping faith with God suddenly break the despicable sin cycle?

Were they able to muster up the discipline they needed to keep their sin in check? Would that have been enough to count their end of the covenant as fulfilled? Could they have added some extra measures onto the 613 laws just to ensure that they were not sinning? Would that have helped? Hmm—couldn't hurt, right? Wrong. Look at the kind of obedience that God required:

> And now, Israel, what does the LORD your God require of you, but to fear the LORD your God, to walk in all his ways, to love him, to serve the LORD your God with all your heart and with all your soul, and to keep the commandments and statutes of the LORD, which I am commanding you today for your good? Behold, to the LORD your God belong heaven and the heaven of heavens, the earth with all that is in it. Yet the LORD set his heart in love on your fathers and chose their offspring after them, you above all peoples, as you are this day. Circumcise therefore the foreskin of your heart, and be no longer stubborn. (Deut. 10:12–16)

As a mom, I often just want sheer conformity from my kids. When I tell them to take responsibility for their chores, I want the chores done. But where does the obedience come from that God is talking about here? God required obedience from the heart. No physical sign (like the sign of circumcision) was ultimately enough. We know what this pattern is pointing us to—the new creation. We need new hearts. For God's people to truly love and obey him, they needed more than rules. They needed new hearts—hearts with his good law written right on them. God had to transform his people from the inside out.

Moses posed the blessings and curses of God to the people. Did the children choose life (Deut. 30:19–20)?

Finally, Settling Down

From Comfort to Captivity

As of this month, our oldest child has been on a record ninety-five airplane flights in her eight years of life. Nobody had to teach her to ask, "Are we there yet?" When you're not there yet, the lagging journey is what your heart tends to stay fixed on. After Moses died on the doorstep of the Promised Land, God commissioned Joshua to be the new leader, promising him, "I will not leave you or forsake you" (Josh. 1:5). The children of Israel were ready to go and were startlingly optimistic: "All that you have commanded us we will do, and wherever you send us we will go" (Josh. 1:16). Don't miss this theme of Yahweh's presence among his people. Watch how this same phrase keeps turning up, and be amazed at the idea of a holy God abiding with sinners like us.

> Be strong and courageous. Do not fear or be in dread of [the nations], for it is the LORD your God who goes with you. He will not leave you or forsake you. . . . It is the LORD who goes

before you. He will be with you; he will not leave you or forsake you. Do not fear or be dismayed. (Deut. 31:6, 8)

Then David said to Solomon his son, "Be strong and courageous and do it. Do not be afraid and do not be dismayed, for the Lord God, even my God, is with you. He will not leave you or forsake you, until all the work for the service of the house of the Lord is finished." (1 Chron. 28:20)

What God commissions, he sees through to the end. He will not forsake us in the work he has given us. As we go and make disciples of all nations, we can be assured of Christ's very presence. "And behold, I am with you always, to the end of the age" (Matt. 28:20). Jesus is with us to the end of the age, because he has gotten rid of our sin and satisfied the wrath of God against us. "*Eli, Eli, lema sabachthani?*" he cried in agony on the cross (Matt. 27:46). Christ took our sin upon himself, and was forsaken on the cross by his Father so we could be with him forever. Until he returns and brings us into the good land of the consummated new creation, we make disciples of all nations. Be strong and very courageous, dear reader. Christ is with you in the good work he has commissioned.

The Mini-Exodus through the Jordan

God wanted his word-dependent nation to be led by a word-filled leader. God instructed Joshua to fill his mind with God's perfect law day and night, to be careful "to do according to all the law that Moses my servant commanded you. Do not turn from it to the right hand or to the left, that you may have good success wherever you go" (Josh. 1:7). The blessing for obedience was certain: "You will make your way prosperous, and then you will have good success" (Josh. 1:8). This is the way of the righteous man. He is the blessed man "who walks not in the counsel of the wicked . . . but his delight is in the law of the Lord, and on his law he mediates day and night. . . . In all that he does, he prospers" (See Ps. 1:1–6). This all sounds so wonderfully ideal, the picture of perfection in paradise. From our fly-over of the Old Testament, the list of God's blessings and curses in Deuteronomy still rings in our ears. But at the same time, the ungratefulness of the people of Israel still leaves a rancid taste in our mouths. Rebellion is bound up in the heart of man, but God commands perfection. As we watch Joshua take up leadership, we wonder if the people will be careful to do all that God has commanded so that they might inherit the land. Would the sons of Adam and the daughters of Eve have their Eden again? Could there be anything better than a land flowing with milk and honey? Weren't there still giants in the land, the giants who had made their parents tremble in their sandals?

In Joshua 3, the ark containing God's word went before the people through the water of the Jordan River. God stacked up the river so that the new generation would have their own mini-exodus, walking through a body of water on dry land. Out of Egypt, out of the wilderness (at last!), and into the Promised Land. Out with the manna in the wilderness and in with the fresh pro-duce of the land (Josh. 5:12). From Jericho to Ai and the Amorites, from Kadesh-barnea to Gaza, and from Goshen to Gibeon—all were given in to their hands when they obeyed the Lord. Joshua repeatedly reminded the people of the Creator's commission in Genesis 1:28: Live by his word, subdue and rule in his name, spread his glory. But when the people disobeyed, they suffered oppression. Some of their enemies still lived among them. Even so, we read in Joshua 21:45 that God remained faithful: "Not one word of all the good promises that the LORD had made to the house of Israel had failed; all came to pass."

Joshua's dying words spark hope and rekindle the great warn-ing against idolatry:

> But just as all the good things that the LORD your God prom-ised concerning you have been fulfilled for you, so the LORD will bring upon you all the evil things, until he has destroyed you from off this good land that the LORD your God has given you, if you transgress the covenant of the LORD your

God, which he commanded you, and go and serve other gods and bow down to them. Then the anger of the Lord will be kindled against you, and you shall perish quickly from off the good land that he has given to you. (Josh. 23:15–16)

Those are sobering last words, aren't they? God's people needed a place where they could finally rest from the chaos inside their hearts. As long as they whored after false gods and turned away from God, they could find no true rest. "You shall perish quickly from off the good land" is a call for sober judgment. In the face of this sobering reality, Joshua makes a bold choice:

But as for me and my house, we will serve the Lord. (Josh. 24:15)

Could there be a grander vision for the purpose of the family than this? Could there be a more epic call to faithfulness for premarital counseling curriculum? Could there be a more perfect verse for calligraphers to inscribe on artwork for newlyweds? Everything in my heart agrees: "Yes! This is what I want for my family!" And it's true; the highest aspiration of every Christian family should be to have this kind of Christ-centered mentality. We were made to live rightly under the King's rule. But every family has their issues, right? Every family wonders, can we *really* be faithful to this call?

Perhaps the Hebrews gave each other knowing glances while they sowed seeds in fields they had taken from their enemies, saying, "Don't mess this up." Perhaps ladies warned their friends of the dangers of admiring their neighbors' pantheon of idols, saying, "Hear, O Israel: The Lord our God, the Lord is one" (Deut. 6:4). Perhaps their hearts beat with promises of God and the remembrance of his faithfulness. Perhaps mothers and fathers took opportunities to instruct their children in the good word of the Lord when they sat in their homes, when they walked along the paths, when they put the kids to bed, and when they ate their breakfast. Perhaps travelers passed through the land, noticed the word of God on their gates, and wondered at these strange people who insisted that God is invisible, he abides no graven images, and he made and keeps a covenant of loyal love with them. Perhaps.

At the end of the book of Joshua we see that Israel was eager to do all that God had said: "The LORD our God we will serve, and his voice we will obey" (Josh. 24:24). Where Adam and Eve failed to serve the Lord and obey his voice, the people said they would succeed. But then, a few verses later, we have to read in between the lines: "Israel served the LORD all the days of Joshua, and all the days of the elders who outlived Joshua and had known all the work that the LORD did for Israel" (Josh. 24:31). Well, hmm. Now that all the leaders whom Joshua had trained were gone, which God would the people serve?

The Next Chapter: Days of Horror

God's story continued. What happened to the optimistic Israelites? Did they resist the gods of the nations among them, those who worshiped the sirens of created images, singing irresistibly to lead them into idolatry? "Choose this day whom you will serve," Joshua challenged the people (Josh. 24:15). But it didn't take very long for the people to forget. Soon, a new generation rose up who did not know the Lord. In Judges 2:10 we read that after that last godly generation of Israelites had died, another generation arose after them who neither knew the Lord nor recognized the work he had done for Israel. In a single generation, their faith was gone. The deadly assumption they made was this: God and his mission do not matter.

A godly heritage was not passed on to them after their parents passed away. The human heart is desperately wicked; the people truly chose *for themselves* whom they would serve. And the family of God fell apart. Individuals, families, and tribes all served idols and forgot about the Lord. It did not matter how many doorposts were inscribed with the laws of God, how many breakfast devotionals they sat through, how many Bible verses their parents trained them to memorize. At the heart of all their religious devotion, they found no pleasure in the Lord. And we must understand this, dear mothering readers: delight in the Lord is not something that we can *give* to our children or disciples. We can only help teach it, suggest it, exemplify it, and affirm it. Salvation belongs to the Lord.

What a relief it is to read the book of Judges in 20/20 hindsight, right? Even as the nation of Israel suffered the consequences for their disobedience to God, they maintained their relentless quest for paradise. But paradise regained is not the inheritance that Yahweh has in mind for his children. Eden rebooted would just end in disaster, again. They needed a new exodus to deliver them once and for all. No earthly, short-term deliverance would do. God wrote eternity on their hearts (Eccles. 3:11), and in their scramble to grab hold of the eternal life that they craved deep down, they settled for the idols of the nations. The cost of such betrayal was high. But God was not wringing his hands. He designed those horrific days, too, to be a pointer to the Judge who would rule perfectly, subdue his enemies totally, and bring the unparalleled blessing of obedience to God's word. The Israelites lived in the land, yes, but there was a better country coming still— a heavenly one (Heb. 11:16). In that place, their longing for God's fullness would be met. But then, even in Canaan, they would live with a homesickness that would be cured only in eternity.

This is the way God has written his story: those who deserve death and eternal punishment receive life by grace. The book of Judges is a record of God's grace to his people. He gave them judge after judge to deliver them from the hands of their enemies. But did his lavish display of forbearing kindness prompt his people to repent? For a little while, yes. But ultimately, no. The final scene in the book depicts the brutal gang rape and murder of a helpless woman. And then the last line of Judges hits us like a ton of bricks:

"In those days there was no king in Israel. Everyone did what was right in his own eyes" (Judg. 21:25).

We who live in countries with some semblance of order cannot fully understand what this is like. The law of the jungle, so to speak, is a mild way to put it. Not a single family in the nation was blameless. These chapters describe the worst of times. We read them and weep. But know that your tears will be mingled with glimmers of hope. As it was in those days of horror, it is today. If you are alive today, no matter how horrible your circumstances, the fact of life is evidence that points to an almighty God's patience and his promise to one day fill the earth with worshipers who worship him in spirit and in truth. You live in the age of unprecedented spiritual fruitfulness through the work of the Spirit, where the obligation of God's people is not *merely* to fill the earth with babies but to multiply faithful image bearers through procreation and discipleship—to reach all the nations with the gospel. God's pattern and promise are in play now. Can you sense the anticipation building? Let's take a look at the book of Ruth.

There's a Bun in the Oven in the House of Bread

Above I mentioned the fact of life. This fact of life, remember, is in contrast to the death that sinners deserve. What would become of the nation of Israel, the people whom God said that he loved because he had chosen to love? Turn the page after Judges, and see where you end up in the canon we affirm as God's holy word. "In the days when the judges ruled . . ." (Ruth 1:1). Oh, boy, here we go again. In the days when the judges ruled, there was a famine in the land. The milk and honey had dried up, and the nation was laid low under the discipline of God.

We are introduced to a man whose name is a little too ironic. Elimelech means "God is King," but this man moved his family *out* of the Promised Land into territory that God, his King, had not given them. In search of life in an attempt to escape death by famine, Elimelech found only death. There in Moab, he died.

His two sons married Gentile women, which was also forbidden. His two sons also died, leaving Elimelech's two daughters-in-law childless. Naomi, the widow, was destitute. Her husband had led the family into certain destruction. But tension mounted in this drama when word got out that Bethlehem, "the house of bread," was restocked and the famine was over (Ruth 1:6). Naomi wanted to go back home, so she urged her Moabite daughters-in-law to go back to their families. Naomi said, "The hand of the LORD has gone out against me" (Ruth 1:13). Our situations may not be as physically desperate as this widow's; she lost everything and was returning to nothing. Yet the delightful irony of Naomi's statement that "the hand of the LORD [was] against [her]," is punctuated with the next verse. Ruth, her Gentile daughter-in-law, "clung to her" (Ruth 1:14).

Knowing the big picture is so helpful for us as mothering women, because we experience times like this, and the people around us experience times like this. In the moment that we believe our God has abandoned us, he is yet holding us fast. God's hand was *not* against Naomi; he was holding her in his grip of grace through Ruth. In moments like these we can sing with Horatio Spafford, a man who lost his son to an illness, his wealth in the Chicago Fire, and his four daughters in a shipwreck, "Whatever my lot, Thou hast taught me to say / 'It is well, it is well, it is well with my soul.'"

Perhaps you know how the story goes. There, in Bethlehem, "the house of bread," Ruth's efforts to provide food for herself and her mother-in-law were guided by the unseen hand of God's good providence. She labored in a barley field and was blessed abundantly by the owner of the field. Boaz, the kinsman redeemer, played his part in rescuing Naomi (and Ruth) from their earthly demise. The child who came from Boaz and Ruth's marriage would be a conduit of grace. The grandson whom Ruth placed in Naomi's lap was none other than Obed, who grew up to be the father of Jesse, the father of David. And from David the shepherd boy would come the greatest Shepherd-King the world has ever seen. But we're getting ahead of ourselves again. Or are we? On seeing the faithfulness of God to the destitute widow, the women of Bethlehem said to Naomi, "Blessed be the LORD, who has not left you this day without a redeemer, and may his name be renowned in Israel!" (Ruth 4:14). And now we, like Naomi, can say because of Yahweh's deliverance that we are "as sorrowful, yet always rejoicing; as poor, yet making many rich; as having nothing, yet possessing everything" (2 Cor. 6:10).

God wrote these people into his story, and their story is also our story. The kinsman-redeemer policies in ancient Israel seem so far off, so foreign. But this is our family tree—all who claim to live by grace through faith in the King are coheirs of the kingdom with these people. In our lineage of faith is a Moabite woman, a Gentile who became part of God's family. The promised "seed of woman" came through—Ruth? This is astonishing. Like Israel in the days when the judges ruled, we face daily temptations to provide for ourselves according to what is right in our own eyes. We taste the dryness of the famine in this fallen world, and we're tempted to abandon the heritage of faith God has given us to seek our own way. We suffer pain and loss, and God lovingly disciplines us as his children, and we conclude that the hand of God is against us. We need eyes to see.

"As for me and my house, we will serve the Lord!" The banner of loyal love to God flies in our hearts. And it flies high because God is faithful to his covenant. Even when we are faithless, his grace keeps us. "If we are faithless, he remains faithful—for he cannot deny himself" (2 Tim. 2:13). The atoning death of the future Shepherd-King is the conclusive evidence. We were still his enemies—subjects who were disloyal to him in every way. Yet it was then that he died for us, to reconcile us to God (Rom. 5:10). Through famine, through exile, and through our return to God, we find grace because of Jesus. And so it is that we continue in the line of faith, obtaining an inheritance by grace just like destitute Naomi.

One King to Rule Them All?

Hannah's womb had been closed by the God in whose hands are the lives of every living thing. In her sorrow, she wept and prayed before the Lord at Shiloh that he might give her a child. In her heartbroken prayers she was not trying to manipulate God but humbly acknowledge her dependence on God. This is the kind of praying that resonates in the heart of every mother: helpless yet hopeful. We pray as J. I. Packer describes in his book *Evangelism and the Sovereignty of God*:

> The prayer of a Christian is not an attempt to force God's hand, but a humble acknowledgement of helpless dependence.[10]

If there is a prayer pounding in your heart, pray it. God is honored by our confession of dependence on and our hope in him. God answered Hannah's prayer when her firstborn son, Samuel, was born, and as she had promised, she dedicated him to service in the tabernacle of God. (His baby dedication was planned before he was ever conceived.) Samuel grew up in the house of the Lord, serving him day and night. What a childhood!

Samuel was a faithful priest. When he grew old, he appointed his two sons to be judges over the people, but they soon became famous in Israel for taking bribes and perverting justice (1 Sam. 8:1–3). Why? Why can't the people just walk in the ways of the Lord? No sooner does a leader rise up and give the people hope, than their fatal flaws are exposed. Samuel failed to restrain his wicked sons. The elders of Israel gathered together and approached Samuel with this demand:

> Behold, you are old and your sons do not walk in your ways. Now appoint for us a king to judge us like all the nations. (1 Sam. 8:5)

They wanted a king. Okay, appointing a king was not forbidden, and Samuel knew this day would one day come (but perhaps not in his lifetime). He knew the laws concerning kings, which Yahweh spoke of before they even conquered the first city in Canaan.

The people's desire for a king was not an odd request. God himself had raised this issue back when Moses was in leadership over the people. One day the people would desire a king, so the Lord gave them instructions for when that day came:

> When you come to the land that the LORD your God is giving you, and you possess it and dwell in it and then say, "I will set a king over me, like all the nations that are around me" . . . (Deut. 17:14)

Kings were to be chosen from among the people (not from among the foreigners). The king was not to "acquire many horses for himself," "acquire many wives for himself," or "acquire for himself excessive silver and gold." He must "learn to fear the LORD his God by keeping all the words of this law and these statutes, and doing them . . . that he may not turn aside from the commandment" (see Deut. 17:16–20). But did there exist among the people such a man as this: a man who would rule and subdue the earth in the name of the Lord, just as Adam should have done? A man who would not turn aside from God's command, either to the right or to the left, just as Adam should have done? A man who would not disqualify himself through greed, immorality, and idolatry? *Oh, that the blessings of God would spill over through his anointed one! Rest on every side! Worldwide worship of Yahweh!* But could there be such a king who would live by every word that proceeds from the mouth of God and usher in God's blessings as *no* man has been able to do at any time in history? Or would such a king only fail, like Adam, and incur further judgment?

It's no wonder that Samuel was dismayed by the elders' request. So he asked the Lord what to do about it. God's answer probably surprised him:

Obey the voice of the people in all that they say to you, for they have not rejected you, but they have rejected me from being king over them. According to all the deeds that they have done, from the day I brought them up out of Egypt even to this day, forsaking me and serving other gods, so they are also doing to you. Now then, obey their voice; only you shall solemnly warn them and show them the ways of the king who shall reign over them. (1 Sam. 8:7–9)

Reluctantly, Samuel anointed Saul as king over Israel as per Yahweh's instruction. Saul started off well, but in time he proved that he was unqualified to rule. His reign was marked by disrespect for God's commands, insistence on his own way, and unbridled jealousy. Israel's first king was an epic failure. It looked as though God's will was not being done on earth as it is in heaven. Like the faithful Israelites who grieved over these events, I think as mothers we can be deeply discouraged over things that look like utter and complete failures. We can forget that God will certainly fulfill his promises in the end. While we rightly grieve the losses we experience in this fallen world, we do not grieve as those without hope. Just watch and see what happens next!

Hallelujah! And He Shall Reign Forever and Ever

And then from the House of Bread, a little shepherd boy was chosen to rule. According to God's instructions, Samuel anointed David to be king even while Saul was still on the throne. The Spirit of the Lord rushed upon David from that day forward (1 Sam. 16:13). His time as king was coming, but it had not yet arrived. God's Enemy knew something was up, so he incited Saul to try to pin the shepherd-king to a wall with his spear. By God's grace, the anointed one escaped time and again from the hand of wicked Saul. For years. *Years!*

But, alas, even David, the man whom God said was "after my heart" (Acts 13:22), was shown to be another son of Adam. His reign was marred by his lust, murder, and failure. Adam's sin has infiltrated us all. Like father, like son. The Philistines surrounded Israel and crept in from time to time. David was not the foretold Serpent crusher. The people faced threats from within and threats from without. And the people faced their sin! From the king to the priests to the people, *who* can stand before the Lord?

That's why 2 Samuel 7 is so astounding. God has been more than patient with the covenant-breaking Israelites. His "kingdom of priests" was perpetually unclean. Instead of mediating God's blessing to the nations and leading them in worship to the one true God, the people continually served the idols of the nations! We're all shaking our heads right now because we see this history repeated even today. God's people are given as a city on the hill to witness to dying people, and we're distracted by the glitter of their gods. There are so many things we could talk about at this point as far as how it relates to our motherhood! For now, let's focus on the fact that we are here because God, in his steadfast, covenant-keeping love, made a promise to David. From his line would come a Son who would be *unlike* Adam. God, who rules over all things and cannot be contained by his creation, would yet dwell with his people. To David he promised, "Your throne shall be established forever" (2 Sam. 7:16). Forever means *forever*. What could David say to that? He knew he did not deserve this grace, yet because of grace, he had the courage to pray, *"Yes and amen"* to all that God promised he would do: "For you, O Lord God, have spoken, and with your blessing shall the house of your servant be blessed forever" (2 Sam. 7:29). Seeing and savoring the supremacy of God would be done on earth as it is done in heaven. But when? Can we please get this party started?

The King Who Would Be Wise

Somewhere around 961 BC, David's son Solomon survived an attempted coup and was established as the rightful king over Israel. Solomon possessed unique, unprecedented, God-given wisdom (1 Kings 10:24). For example, Solomon had specifically requested of God the ability to discern between good and evil, that he might judge the people well (1 Kings 3:4–9).[11] Whereas Adam deceptively tried to acquire the knowledge of good and evil and was judged for it, Solomon directly asked God for such wisdom, and it pleased the Lord to grant it to him.

Solomon built a glorious temple to replace the tabernacle, adorning it with garden images overlaid with gold. As a result, no longer was there the need for a temporary place for God's ark and his presence, but a permanent building. It was a dazzling sight to behold! Gold was everywhere, and it is mentioned at least thirty times in the account of Solomon's kingship. His wisdom even extended to unique areas such as animal husbandry, gardening, and forestry. (Does this remind you of someone else who was God's special vice-regent?)[12] The people of Israel *multiplied* "as many as the sand by the sea" (1 Kings 4:2). He "excelled all the kings of the earth in riches and in wisdom. And the whole earth sought the presence of Solomon to hear his wisdom, which God had put into his mind" (1 Kings 10:23–24). Nations—*the whole earth*—came into Solomon's presence to be blessed. Are you getting excited yet?

The people were happy, too. Specifically, they ate and drank and were happy (1 Kings 4:20). Peace, abundance, and feasting were their new normal. Could this be the eternal kingdom of God's consummated blessings? I hate to say this, but take a closer look back at 1 Kings 10:14–29 and we get a hint of what is about to happen. Against the commands of the Lord in Deuteronomy 17, Solomon was busy acquiring many horses from Egypt, many wives for himself from among the nations, and silver and gold for his treasury. Solomon's heart was not fully God's. He did not love the Lord his God with all his heart, soul, mind, and strength. In 1 Kings 11, the downward spiral is detailed: Solomon clung to one thousand women who turned his heart away from the Lord. His idolatry was profuse, and he built temples and altars for his foreign wives to worship demons. "So Solomon did what was evil in the sight of the LORD and did not wholly follow the LORD, as

David his father had done" (1 Kings 11:6). He led the people of Israel astray, whoring after images of created things. All the while, everybody was eating, drinking, and enjoying happiness. Only heaven knows how many of God's image bearers were sacrificed to Satan in those days, under the reign of the king who wanted to be wise.

Under the rule of Solomon's sons, the kingdom of Israel split into northern and southern tribes, each with their own kings. The nation of kingly priests unto the Lord was no more—they were divided and becoming increasingly pagan. The people in the northern tribes rejected God, and they were carried away into exilic captivity by the Assyrians (722 BC). The people in the southern tribes also rejected God, and they were carried away into exilic captivity by the Babylonians (586 BC). Jerusalem fell to the nations, and the temple was destroyed.

Psalm 72, a psalm that was written by (or for) Solomon, speaks of days that never fully came to pass under his reign. Can you imagine what kind of king could command this kind of rule?

Give the king your justice, O God,
and your righteousness to the royal son! (v. 1)

May he defend the cause of the poor of the people,
give deliverance to the children of the needy,
and crush the oppressor! (v. 4)

May he have dominion from sea to sea,
and from the River to the ends of the earth! (v. 8)

May all kings fall down before him,
all nations serve him! (v. 11)

He has pity on the weak and the needy,
and saves the lives of the needy.
From oppression and violence he redeems their life,
and precious is their blood in his sight. (vv. 13–14)

> May his name endure forever,
>> his fame continue as long as the sun!
> May people be blessed in him,
>> all nations call him blessed! (v. 17)

> Blessed be [the LORD's] glorious name forever;
>> may the whole earth be filled with his glory! (v. 19)

Those are all promises that were coming; the stage was set. It sure did look like deliverance was finally on its way through a few of those kings. But the Serpent-crushing, justice-giving, nations-blessing, nations-ruling, righteous, royal Son was not here yet. Now, with the kingdom of Israel divided, the people exiled, and their land occupied, would the King have a kingdom to rule when he finally arrived?

6

Mission Rebooted

From Exile to Return to Kingdom

We're still flying fast and high over the old, old story. God's patterns are being revealed, and his promises are being given. This tapestry of grace is astonishing, exciting, and beautiful. And the cross! We can see the cross looming large on the horizon. But when will we see *him*—high and lifted up and exalted (Isa. 52:13)? How will Jesus accomplish his will through us as we mother others according to his pattern, holding onto his promises? Those answers are coming soon! Let's take a closer look at this last epoch in the Old Testament.

The nation of Israel was in disarray. Even though faithful kings entered the story here and there, the main plot for the nation of Israel was marked by division and wicked kings. In spite of this national confusion, the prophets and their ministry held out the word of God as the standard and rule. It may have seemed like every man and king was on stage for himself, but *God* is always sovereign over the script. He is the sovereign to whom all flesh owe their allegiance. He will not give his glory to another. The sins of the nation were grievous, and the prophets exposed their sins in the spotlight of truth. God raised up prophets to cry out woes of judgment and hold out God's promises. Remember the Lord! Remember the Lord!

Elijah preached, rebuked kings and queens, and prophesied. Hosea showed the people a living parable of God's relentless love toward his prostitute wife, the descendants of Abraham. Jonah was sent to Nineveh, sailed the other way, and was graciously rerouted through a three-day trip in a God-ordained, fish-belly ride.

But the people, on the whole, did not repent. The poor among them were trampled. Widows and orphans were left to die by the wayside. The wealthy made themselves fat without regard to the suffering at their gates. Kings ruled to their own advantage. So God used the superpowers of the day—nations in the hand of God—to carry his people away out of their land and into captivity. The Assyrians took Israel from the land in the north. Babylonians conquered Judah in the south. During this time, Micah and Isaiah prophesied of God's judgment for the people's hypocritical worship. The consequences for their repudiation of God's ways and their blatant idolatry would be grave:

> Hear this, you heads of the house of Jacob
>   and rulers of the house of Israel,
> who detest justice
>   and make crooked all that is straight,
> who build Zion with blood
>   and Jerusalem with iniquity. . . .
> Therefore because of you
>   Zion shall be plowed as a field;
> Jerusalem shall become a heap of ruins,
>   and the mountain of the house a wooded height.
>   (Mic. 3:9–10, 12)

Did you get a sense of the nausea this news must have invoked? The peace and prosperity that the nation had enjoyed under Solomon were now but a memory.

Distant Memories of Peace

It was a Monday morning in captivity, and the people were shackled to a pagan nation, expats in a foreign land and deprived of the temple worship that they depended upon as sacrifices for their sins. Just another day in exile. The people woke up every day and went to bed every night—lost.

The remnant would have to learn that their home was not their refuge. The Lord was their refuge. We, too, as "aliens and strangers" in a world that is passing away, need to learn that *our home is not our refuge; God is our refuge.* We nurture life in the face of death and leverage our homes for gospel work. For those whose hope is in the coming kingdom, our homes are less like retreats and more like a network of foxholes for planning and hosting kingdom advances into this present darkness. Our homes are centers of hospitality to show strangers and neighbors the light of Christ. And they are equipping centers for traveling ambassadors to help them on their way to doing the King's business.

Into the darkness and lostness of exile, Yahweh's words of hope rang out through the prophets. Here are just a few of those words. Can you recognize Jesus in these passages?

> But you, O Bethlehem Ephrathah,
> who are too little to be among the clans of Judah,
> from you shall come forth for me
> one who is to be ruler in Israel,
> whose coming forth is from of old,
> from ancient days. (Mic. 5:2)

> And I will place on his shoulder the key of the house of David. He shall open, and none shall shut; and he shall shut, and none shall open. (Isa. 22:22)

> I will give them a heart to know that I am the LORD, and they shall be my people and I will be their God, for they shall return to me with their whole heart. (Jer. 24:7)

The people surely thought, *How could these things be?* Bethlehem was overrun. The house of David had no power. And the people were rightly disciplined for their sin of not loving the Lord their God with all their heart. They had never been able to return to the Lord, not fully anyway. God's promises were getting ramped up higher and higher. Would he fulfill every word spoken to them? Or were the prophets as delusional as some of the people said they were?

After all, the kings and elders continually resisted the prophets' teaching and found ways to put them to death. Should the people believe the prophets? Or did the prophets die in vain, holding onto empty promises and believing their overactive religious imaginations? I've talked with people today who hold this view of God's word: overactive religious imagination. They cite science and wonder if religious people have some kind of genetic disorder. They think that when those genes get twisted too hard, they create an annoying fundamentalist. Or worse, a violent terrorist. What does the world do with people who hold onto their belief in the unseen?

Through Fire and through Lions

Being caught in our sin and called to repentance is God's grace to us, but we don't always see it that way. In most instances, Israel didn't repent when the prophets called out the people's sins. But something different happened during King Josiah's reign. Repentance was widespread throughout Judah after King Josiah reformed the temple back to the worship of Yahweh. (His grandfather, King Manasseh, had adapted the temple into an idol's paradise.) Josiah got rid of the idols that were set up in the temple. In one sense, the people were now worshiping God in truth, but it cost them everything—specifically, all of their idols. We would do well to consider their example. How hard it must have been to chop up that first idol! "Are we sure about this? Shall we hang onto a relic just in case Yahweh isn't enough?" It's humbling to think of how often we make this kind of reasoning in our own hearts. Again, Packer is helpful here in understanding a particular connection between repentance and faith. When we speak with our children, friends, and neighbors and urge them to have faith in Christ, we can't pretend it is cheap grace and that they are welcome to hold on to their idols. "In common honesty, we must not conceal the fact that free forgiveness in one sense will cost everything."[13]

It cost the Israelites everything they had previously clung to in order to worship God in truth. But even in the newfound worship of God, the people still had issues. Jeremiah spoke as the Lord spoke to him, rebuking Israel's sin and warning them of the coming Babylonian invasion. Jeremiah also spoke about the coming days when God would make a new covenant that was unlike the covenant that faithless Israel had broken.

But to the people, news of a new covenant sounded too good to be true. And no wonder—have you read Jeremiah's Lamentations about the invasion? Devastation was on every side, but Jeremiah knew something that stoked the fires of his faith. Where is his hope?

> But this I call to mind,
>   and therefore I have hope:
> The steadfast love of the LORD never ceases;
>   his mercies never come to an end;
> they are new every morning;
>   great is your faithfulness.
> "The LORD is my portion," says my soul,
>   "therefore I will hope in him." (Lam. 3:21–24)

And it's always morning somewhere, isn't it? Jeremiah preached life in the face of death. It was evident that no one was faithful except the Lord. The people had no reason to expect anything but more judgment, because, after all, they certainly deserved it. Lest they presume upon the grace of God, Jeremiah made it clear that God would not be presumed upon. These following verses are ones we cite all the time, but do you see now how they are baffling and beyond imagination? This new covenant was, well, *new*. It was new in every way. Does this description sound familiar to you?

> For this is the covenant that I will make with the house of Israel after those days, declares the LORD: I will put my law within them, and I will write it on their hearts. And I will be their God, and they shall be my people. And no longer shall each one teach his neighbor and each his brother, saying, "Know the LORD," for they shall all know me, from the least of them to the greatest, declares the LORD. For I will forgive their iniquity, and I will remember their sin no more. (Jer. 31:33–34)

In the midst of end-time deception, the Spirit of God would unleash end-time restoration. Yet through an age of corruption from within and persecution from without, Yahweh will keep for himself a remnant. These people will see their mourning turned into joy, and they will be satisfied with his goodness.

This better, new covenant would be mediated by Christ, our Great High Priest, and made with "eschatological Israel," the elect Jewish remnant and elect Gentiles. It is these few who are the "true Israel" by grace through faith. For these "the LORD has prepared a sacrifice and consecrated his guests" (Zeph. 1:7). The ram caught in the thicket, the scapegoat sent into the wilderness, the Passover lamb: all these patterns pointed to a once-for-all sacrifice for sin. The blood that speaks a better word than the blood of Abel is the blood of Christ (Heb. 12:24).

So what does the world do with people who are willing to die for their belief in God and insist on his truth? Well, actually, the world does know what to do with people who are willing to die for their beliefs. Conspire against them. Pass legislation to trap them. Throw them into the fire. Throw them to the lions (Daniel

3; 6). Daniel and his faithful compatriots in Babylon survived the attempts against their lives by casting themselves on the mercy of God. The fourth man in the fire stood with them, and he sent his angels to shut the mouths of lions. God miraculously preserved the remnant, keeping them for himself. The same holds true even as the spirit of the Antichrist that Daniel prophesied about persuades many to disregard God, scorn his holiness, and cling to false doctrine. The apostle Paul said that "the mystery of lawlessness is already at work" (2 Thess. 2:7). This kind of mystery isn't a classic whodunit mystery but a surprising revelation that was previously unseen or expected. The end-time tribulation that Daniel spoke of will persist during the church age. Deceptive false teachers are working now, though the incarnate Antichrist has not yet appeared to "exalt himself and magnify himself above every god" in view of the worldwide church (Dan. 11:36). At that time persecution will spread far and wide, the temple will be desecrated, and false teachers will spout their lies from within the covenant community.[14] Let the reader understand.

Ezekiel prophesied, and as Jerusalem fell, the people were taken into captivity in Babylon. Although life in Babylon wasn't too terrible for most of them (with the exception of a few fire-walking faithful Jews and a man who was thrown to the lions for praying to God), still the people could not worship Yahweh in the way he had prescribed. I know many people today who live like this, even in a place that feels to them like "home." Sometimes expat life does not feel like exile, but the people get comfortable among the nations and think they are home. But a better home is coming. Keep watching! The Spirit would give life to their souls, and one day the valley of dry bones would be raised up from the dust.

There's No Place Like Home?

In 539 BC, Babylon was taken by the Medo-Persians. Then Cyrus allowed the Jews to go back home to set up their own province under his leadership. The king's heart was in the hand of the Lord, and he sent the Jews back to Judea so they could rebuild their temple. Despite opposition from the locals, and despite the fact that some of the remnant chose not to return, the temple was rebuilt in Jerusalem. But it wasn't the same as before. You can see that all the restoration prophecies were beginning to be fulfilled, but you can also see that the restoration work the people did was imperfect. The new temple, as wonderful as it was for many, was "less than." The older generation knew this, and they wailed. The people were disappointed and disaffected but, nonetheless, eager to worship the Lord.

Later, Nehemiah would be dispatched from his exile to go back home and rebuild the walls of the city. A pagan king gave what was needed to do this massive work. A young Jewish woman, Esther, was chosen out of an entire harem to have an audience with the Persian king. God's unseen hand guided her heroic work through the most remarkable circumstances, and she saved her people from racism-fueled genocide (Esther 8). It wouldn't be the last time they were marked for death because of their ethnicity.

Hundreds of years later, in 63 BC, Pompey the Great ignored a tangled web of political quandaries swirling around him and rashly marched up to Jerusalem to try to take Judea from the Persians. He noted the ominous task before him:

> For he saw the walls were so firm, that it would be hard to overcome them; and that the valley before the walls was terrible; and that the temple, which was within that valley, was itself encompassed with a very strong wall, insomuch that if the city were taken, that temple would be a second place of refuge for the enemy to retire to.[15]

The Jews refused to surrender and barricaded themselves in a portion of the city. After a three-month siege, Pompey's troops invaded the Jews' stronghold and massacred twelve thousand people. They desecrated the temple and barged into the Most Holy Place, where only the high priest was allowed. "Pay tribute or die," they decreed to all who remained in Judea. The kingdom, as the nation of Israel knew it, was lost. Could Isaiah's promise really come to pass?

> For behold, I create new heavens
> > and a new earth,
> and the former things shall not be remembered
> > or come into mind. (Isa. 65:17)

Where was the Lord, while his temple was being desecrated and his ark being carried away by an idolatrous army?

> The sound of an uproar from the city!
> > A sound from the temple!
> The sound of the LORD,
> > rendering recompense to his enemies! (Isa. 66:6)

The Jews were shuffled over to the rule of the Romans. Their pagan gods were an outrage to the Jews. Some were weary of living under such conditions. Some learned to just accept their lot and completely forgot to look for the Serpent crusher. After all, God had not spoken to them for four hundred years. *Four hundred years.* Long gone were people who knew people who had heard a prophet speak the words of Yahweh. Had God forgotten about them? Where was their deliverer?

But, O holy night. While long lay the world in sin and error pining, he appeared. A thrill of hope! The weary soul rejoices! For yonder breaks a new and glorious morn.[16]

Fall on Your Knees

In the province of Judea, around 4 BC, during the reign of Caesar Augustus, into the darkness *the* light dawned. A virgin was overshadowed by the Holy Spirit, and God conceived his Son through the seed of a woman. But the darkness heard about the light and sought to snuff him out. Satan incited the hatred of King Herod, and he unleashed a specific infanticide on the Jewish community, ordering that their baby boys be extinguished in a night. Rachel's tears were already counted by the Lord, who had said several hundred years earlier,

> A voice is heard in Ramah, lamentation and bitter weeping. Rachel is weeping for her children; she refuses to be comforted for her children, because they are no more. (Jer. 31:15; cf. Matt. 2:13–18)

But there was one baby boy who escaped the sword of Herod. All the angels of heaven stood ready at the command of the Lord to shield his Anointed, and the Father dispatched a winged warrior to warn Joseph of Herod's coming slaughter. Into the night the boy, his mother, and his adoptive father fled to Egypt. This, too, was according to God's plan: "When Israel was a child, I loved him, and out of Egypt I called my son" (Hos. 11:1).

Jesus increased in wisdom and in stature and in favor with God and man (Luke 2:52). At every point of contention with the Serpent, this last Adam was victorious. At no point did he succumb to the Devil's temptations to worship him. By the Spirit of God, he cast out demons, proving that the kingdom of God was at last breaking in to the old age (Matt. 12:28).

Because he is the Son of God, and only God can do this, Jesus offered eternal life. Jesus made an offer that no prophet, priest, or king could ever give. He fulfilled the law that Moses and the priests had mediated but could not follow. He brought kingdom blessings and set up the eternal throne that David failed to do because of his sin. And Adam. Oh, Adam. Jesus, the firstfruits from the dead, has in himself everyone who would be born after his kind. Whereas everyone in Adam shall die, everyone in Christ shall live (1 Cor. 15:22). Who can fulfill a promise like this? Only Christ.

> The light has come into the world, and people loved the darkness rather than the light because their works were evil. (John 3:19)

According to their sin and according to the eternal plan of God, they put the Son of Man to death on a cross. But what man and Satan meant for evil, the triune God meant for good from eternity past. You see, there on the cross, God made him who knew no sin to become sin for us, so that we could become the righteousness of God (2 Cor. 5:21). The Father was pleased to pour out his wrath on his Son—for us. The obedient Son of Man, who had set his face toward Jerusalem from before time began, took a fatal fang in the foot while he crushed the Serpent's head. He died, was buried, and was left for dead in a garden tomb. The promised seed of the woman was put into the ground.

Go, Tell It on the Mountain

But three days later, everything changed. The old passed away, and the new came. In a moment in the garden, the new creation dawned. And it happened in such a way that people needed to be told. We still need to be told. "The light shines in the darkness, and the darkness has not overcome it" (John 1:5).

Listen! All who would be taken out of Adam and placed in the last Adam will be living, breathing, walking new creations in him (2 Cor. 5:17). God's image bearers, newly created in the image of God's beloved Son, are now walking, talking, serving, living, and dying in Christ's name. They are the church, that pan-ethnic nation of priests who make living sacrifices acceptable to God in the outer court of the world. Their witness is a light to the nations: you don't need to come to a temple with a lamb to sacrifice; you need to become part of the sacrificed Lamb's temple.

Christ commissioned his followers to go into all the world, baptizing and teaching men, women, and children from every nation to obey all that he commanded. The Master of the house is coming back, and he has left his stewards in charge of doing his will while he is away. "Behold, I am coming soon, bringing my recompense with me, to repay each one for what he has done,"

Jesus said (Rev. 22:12). And then the total package of the new creation and resurrection life will be delivered—a world without end. Amen.

Gentiles, too, will be brought into the kingdom, joined together with Jewish believers in Christ's body, the church. Though this inclusion was a surprise to many, it was always in God's heart:

> "And the foreigners who join themselves to the LORD,
>   to minister to him, to love the name of the LORD,
>   and to be his servants,
> everyone who keeps the Sabbath and does not profane it,
>   and holds fast my covenant—
> these I will bring to my holy mountain,
>   and make them joyful in my house of prayer;
> their burnt offerings and their sacrifices
>   will be accepted on my altar;
> for my house shall be called a house of prayer
>   for all peoples."
> The Lord GOD,
>   who gathers the outcasts of Israel, declares,
> "I will gather yet others to him
>   besides those already gathered." (Isa. 56:6–8)

By the grace of God, the Gentiles are the "other sheep that are not of this fold" who were brought in when they heard the Shepherd's voice (John 10:16). The other lost sheep will hear his voice too. And they will listen. We have this great assurance in our mission to disciple the nations.

So here we are, at the end of part 1. The new age has broken into the old age. So part 2 on missional motherhood, which describes God's promises played out, is ready to break into part 1. (See what I did there?)

We need a hero. Here is the Savior to whom every mother needs to look:

> For all the promises of God find their Yes in him. That is why
> it is through him that we utter our Amen to God for his glory.
> (2 Cor. 1:20)

How is Jesus the Yes and Amen to all of God's promises? What
does he mean to us as nurturers? How on earth will Jesus bring
about his heavenly kingdom? How will he use our missional motherhood? How will Jesus keep God's promises to us—promises that
we are banking on in our everyday ministry of motherhood?

We've now taken a sweeping tour of the Old Testament. Hopefully the altitude of this big-picture perspective hasn't left you
feeling dizzy! As we go and mother disciples, let's keep tracking
together as we explore further into the dawning kingdom of God's
pattern and promises being played out through Christ himself.

Part 2

THE EVERYDAY
MINISTRY OF
MOTHERHOOD

Go, Therefore, and Mother Disciples

7

Christ, the Creator of Motherhood

My hope for part 1 was that we would see that we are not truly central to the big story. *God is central.* I've prayed that you and all the women who read the first half of this book would feel appropriately small, dependent, *decentralized*, and yet, in a God-centered way, *significant.* As we talked about in the introduction, the God who existed before time did not create anything meaningless. Through the person and work of Jesus Christ, we will see God's pattern played out perfectly and his promises fulfilled. The purpose of part 2 is to keep pounding this drum in every chapter: missional motherhood is about Jesus.

I think we mothers—biological and spiritual—tend to feel that we are pretty central. I'm not at all saying that as a put-down but as an observation of my own life and the lives of the women I know. An older African woman in our church is surrounded by the women she disciples the moment she walks into the foyer of the hotel ballroom where we gather for corporate worship. An Asian pastor's wife is bombarded by requests and affection from her three sons (especially before dinnertime). A woman in the East Asian community of our church has a virtually 24/7 ministry to the young ladies who sit in her living room to soak in sweet fellowship. My point is this: the people in our lives know where to go for food, protection, and help. They know where to go to grow. They come to *you*, mothering woman, for provision. No pressure, right? Thankfully, we know that God is the one who is faithful to provide what they need.

When I say that we feel central, part of the reason is that sometimes we are, literally, central. Think of a swirling group of kindergarteners who flock to their teacher when the bell rings. Think of the young ladies who watch the doors of your church building, scanning the crowd for *her* to arrive—the older mother hen who mothers the single women. Think of the weary new moms who gravitate toward the older moms with questions, concerns, and prayer requests. Nurturers are in the middle of it all, surrounded by needs. They are conduits of God's grace, just as he designed them to be. Of course mothering women tend to feel central.

Peculiar Dragon's-Blood Trees and Worshipers Purchased by Christ's Precious Blood

To introduce the main point of this chapter, I want to tell you about a spectacular island near the Arabian Peninsula. Tucked nearly out of sight from the rest of the world, the tiny island of Socotra sits on the Gulf of Aden near the shores of Yemen and Somalia. More than seven hundred species of flora and fauna, including peculiar dragon's-blood trees, goofy-looking cucumber trees, and scores of endangered birds enchant visiting biologists. Our Creator displays his incomparable wisdom in the island's unique biodiversity.

But there's a creation on that island that is more ingenious than the Seussical-looking plants and lovelier than the exotic animals. Around 100,000 image bearers of the one, true God live on Socotra. The indigenous Al-Mahrah tribe (of Arab descent) are currently an unreached people group, meaning they have little to no access to the gospel of Jesus Christ. The Lamb who was slain from before the foundation of the world is worthy of the Socotran's worship. Everyone wants to come see their dragon's-blood trees, but Jesus has purchased worshipers from that tribe with his precious blood. How will they hear this good news unless someone tells them? How will people tell them unless they get up and go? I like how Packer explains our task plainly for our understanding:

> God's way of saving men is to send out his servants to tell them the gospel, and the Church has been charged to go into all the world for that very purpose.[17]

Pray the Lord of the harvest would send workers to spread his fame in Socotra. My husband and I like to joke (though it's not really a joke) that there is no such thing as a bored missionary. Everyone on the field wants and needs coworkers for the harvest, regularly praying that God would send them more help. Pray that the Lord would raise up workers who help equip and send more workers!

As astonishingly beautiful as the world is, God's most valuable creation are his image bearers. Without this foundational truth, missional motherhood doesn't exist. If Christ did not create motherhood, then the mission of motherhood devolves into a foolhardy attempt to delay our inevitable death. In cultures where Christ's intentions for motherhood are not valued, they believe either that motherhood is to be avoided at all costs or that motherhood is to be worshiped.

How does the concept of Christ's creation of motherhood change our perspective? That's the question we're digging into in this chapter.

Motherhood and the Meaning of Life

You are here because God made you and sustains your life by the word of his power. He filled the earth with good things for you to enjoy. The provisions you have—by the sweat of your own brow or someone else's—are ultimately the result of his benevolence. In the middle of his good creation, the Creator placed his very good, animated icons. Human life is the result of God's intentional plan, which is no trivial, ignorable thing. His plan then and his plan now are to glorify himself in all the cosmos. For God to be the supreme deity, he *must* value his glory above all things. For him to do otherwise would be idolatrous.[18] God does this by satisfying us with himself forever. He wants us to see that he is the supreme beauty to admire and the supreme person to love. And he doesn't want us just to see these things, but also to taste these truths. What good is it to only look at honey? You have to eat it to fully enjoy it.

God has an unimpeachable plan to make himself known, and he has designed God-centered roles for his image bearers to play. But ever since the cosmic collapse in the garden of Eden, when our first parents sinned, we women have been nurturing life in the face of *death*.

Janet, a single woman who works at the laundry downstairs in a corner of the grocery store, left her home country to find work. She works twelve-hour shifts six days a week and lives in a one-bedroom apartment with fifteen other women. They've all moved to this city for the same purpose: to earn money in order to send it home to feed hungry mouths, to build homes, and to care for aging parents. Amy, a woman who lives in our apartment building, fled her home country just before their dictator was removed from power and executed. She is thankful to live in this peaceable country with her husband and four children, and elated that her kids can attend school without fear. I'll never forget the morning we heard that President Obama had been reelected. I was visiting with Amy when the news was announced on her television. She turned to me and said, "Congratulations on your country's peaceful election. Everyone can vote without being slaughtered on the way."[19]

My friends do not know Jesus (yet). Though they feel some incentive to live for the next world, the particular afterlife they are hoping for exists only in their imagination. Day in and day out, they're just living for another day and another way to provide for the ones they love. This is a noble mission. But the mission of their sacrificial nurturing work would be radically reoriented if they understood that Christ is the creator of motherhood. Motherhood is for his purposes in the world.

It is Christ's image that we are to embody as we plant the fields, judge the cases, fly the planes, organize the data, paint the paintings, feed the hungry, sweep the kitchen, pave the roads, diaper the babies, build the cities—and resist evil. As we embody Christ's image, we point to him. In the minutes it took you to read those few paragraphs above, billions of image bearers received God's common grace as they walked through their days. Some woke up to a new day to see that the sun has risen *again*. Some fell asleep under a sky filled with stars, smog, monsoon rain, or dust *again*. We're all God's dependent creatures, nurturing life in the face of death. God designed his creation to praise him, and his creation of motherhood is no exception.

But the vast majority of people do not know this. They go about their days and nights believing the pagan lie that life is food and clothing (Matt. 6:25–34). And then they die. We know about the *bios* of life, according to the wisdom of the age and our cultural preferences. We know about the *goodness* of life, according to the images we've been shown since we were babies. But do we embody the *zoe* kind of life? Jesus's definition of eternal life is centered on knowing something:

> And this is eternal life, that they know you the only true God, and Jesus Christ whom you have sent. (John 17:3)

God Reserves the Right to Design Motherhood

Here's a bit of a spoiler for the conclusion. Christ created motherhood for himself. Since God is the creator and we are the created, God is the one who gets to design motherhood. In part 1 we saw how God, who is before all things, in his infinite wisdom chose to create man and woman. He created us different, yet similar; equal in dignity, but unequal in role. But it is crucial that we not read "unequal" as synonymous with a scale of importance or value. Unequal, in this case, simply means "not the same." Both sexes—male and female—are not the same, *and* both men and women are created in the image of God. The gender-specific roles we both play are different, but the God-glorifying purpose is the same. The way a woman feeds and protects life is different from the way a man feeds and protects life. Sociology, history, biology, empirical observation, and theology all tell us this.

Expressions of male and female nurturing of life vary from culture to culture. Here's a brief example from where we live. When my kids see an older local man walking toward them on the sidewalk, they know they might receive a pat on the head, a blessing, a piece of candy, some coins, or all of the above. (Yes, kids get paid for being kids here. It's no college fund, to be sure, but it's enough to pay for a chocolate milk.) When I ventured out to the grocery store for the first time with my four kids, my tiny newborn cried in the checkout line. The woman in front of us and the woman behind us argued over who would get to hold the squalling infant. The older woman won the argument, and I gladly passed her my baby so I could unload my grocery cart onto the counter and pay the cashier. She tucked my baby's sweaty little head under her chin, looped her shawl over his body, and whispered a sweet song in her heart language into his ear. Now, of course men can sing to babies, and women can bless children with their words and treats from their purse. If you look around you, you'll notice many more ways that men and women serve and protect the lives around them, and generally speaking, from culture to culture, men and women nurture life differently.

So be encouraged in your mothering. God has designed you to serve him in an intentional and necessary way. Of course, *he* doesn't need you, but he has designed us to need each other. God is self-sufficient, and he created human beings with a need to know him. He placed them in a world full of things that show his invisible attributes, namely, his eternal power and divine nature (Rom. 1:20). He walked with Adam and Eve and gave them his words to live by. But he also sits on a throne surrounded by six-winged seraphim and unspeakably amazing heavenly beings who praise him day and night. He created human life in his image; so smile, mom. Because God is profound, his design for your motherhood is profound.

God Designed Women to Mother According to His Image

But because we live "east of Eden" (see Gen. 3:24), we imagers are tempted to worship created things instead of God. We're tempted to exchange the glory of God for something less than God, which is idolatry. God designed us to display the image of his beloved Son, but our lives get hijacked by the evil powers and principalities that stand in opposition to God. The course of this world is hell-bent against your imaging Christ.

You've likely heard the phrase "image is everything." Our history supplies ample evidence that we are image-embodying creatures, from ancient tribal people who built totem poles of animal images, to models on a runway in Milan dressed in a designer's finest, to soldiers wearing a customized uniform, and to housewives filling their cupboards with a special brand of food stuff. We can't help but image *something*. My daughter doesn't want to represent anything she considers "babyish." My son wants to emulate Spider-Man. I just want to embody comfort. (Is it time for a coffee break? And why does exercise have to involve sweat? Is there a way I can do all these things without making tough choices and sacrifices? Sign me up for whatever gig that is.)

So here are two big questions for us who believe that Christ created motherhood:

1. Do I live out the idea that "image is everything" in my mothering?
2. Does my mothering demonstrate that the imaged One is everything?

The answers to those questions are important, because they reveal who we are pointing to in our work. Since Jesus Christ is the Creator of motherhood, the mission of motherhood is to glorify him. Certainly, you see your own face when you look in the mirror, but what is it that you want other people to see when they look at you? Your stuff? Your work? Your marriage? Your body? Your children? Your everyday ministry? Your disciples? Your accessories? These are tough questions, but we have to ask them because of who God is. We have no authority above the living God. The priority of worshiping him in Spirit and in truth stands above human reasoning, scientific beliefs, theological opinions, church traditions, cultural consensus, and everything else. It is no subissue to question the images we show forth in our lives.

Why do we ask these painful questions about our sin? Are we legalists, trying to pull ourselves up by moralistic bootstraps? By no means. We press in to these questions *not* because we can reach a point of perfection where we can say, "At last! I've done it. I am pointing to God perfectly in everything I do." No, we press in to these questions because we need to see how thoroughly perfect *Christ* is in pointing to himself. At the foot of the cross, the sin of exalting ourselves is not damning to us, because we look up and see the Man who bore that sin away as far as the east is from the west. We are not threatened by the prospect of seeing our sin; we are thrilled by the gospel of grace that says we can repent of our sin because Christ has broken its power over us. We examine our hearts by grace through faith, we identify our sins by grace through faith, we confess our sins to one another by grace through faith, we repent of our sins by grace through faith, and we encourage one another to run the race with endurance by grace through faith.

So, what are some of the particular ways that God's design for us to image his Son gets hijacked? How does Jesus reclaim the glory that is rightly his? For the sake of space, I'll just point out one thing: consumerism.

God Designed Women to Mother While Consuming His Word

Recall from part 1 how God created Adam and Eve to be word-dependent creatures. They were to live in accordance with the reality that "man lives by every word that comes from the mouth of the LORD" (Deut. 8:3). But recall how, as my friends Shai and Blair Linne have put it, Adam and Eve "chose to eat the lie."[20] Satan has offered everyone the same lie, from the patriarchs and Israel to Jesus and his disciples. Satan is not innovative. He works to convince men and women to live by every word that comes from his mouth instead of from God's. The Devil knows that the Creator designed us to be consumers, so he works to get us to feast on things other than God. Satan leverages the course of this world to fill us up with the world rather than allow us to be filled with the Spirit.

Consumerism is an idolatrous preoccupation with stuff. But consumerism is not limited to wealthy Western women in the suburbs. You can be a Dalit mom living in a slum in Mumbai and still be eaten alive by consumerism. Consumerism has less to do with how much stuff you have; it has to do with how much affection your heart has for stuff. The basic premise is this: you can own stuff, but does your stuff own you?

Perhaps you feel the tug in your heart to consume things. You see an eight-second commercial and suddenly you feel deprived, wondering if you need that thing being advertised. You notice a woman wearing something that piques your interest, and you picture yourself in that thing. Your friend's child was given a gift for her birthday, and you imagine your own child having it. You scroll through Facebook and get hungry for others' images—their lunch, their earrings, their tea, their body shape, their vacation sunset, and their *life*. Satan is the architect of the course of this world, and he reinforces the lie that you do not need to live by every word that comes from the mouth of the Lord. He tells you the lie that your life cannot *possibly* amount to more than food and clothing; the lie that only idiots forgo treasure on earth for treasure in heaven; the lie that the real fool is the one who does *not* worry about tomorrow; the lie that if you seek the kingdom of God and his righteousness, you will be sorely disappointed.

That's how it works. Train the consumer to consume temporary fillers. Tell her to collect the tokens that assure her that she has what she needs. Tell her to seek joy in learning that home remedy, buying that decoration, rearranging that schedule, enrolling her kids in that program, or building herself up into the image that she wants to embody. All of those things are easy enough to do if you have enough money, discipline, time, energy, or earthly resources.

But there's a catch: collecting the tokens and living by the lie that your image will give you the peace you crave will only satisfy you for a moment. And then you need another fix. Idols need dusting and maintaining. They always leave you wanting something more, something better, something new, or something your neighbor has. Consuming, we are consumed. When the gods of this world leverage our needs and redirect our hope away from God himself, they indirectly hinder our obedience to the Great Commission. How many missionaries have been held back by consumerism's short leash? (We can't afford to go.) How many of our giving budgets have been strangled by consumerism's shortsighted vision? (We can't afford to give.) How many of our families have been capped by consumeristic spending forecasts? (We can't afford to grow.) We need the promises of Jesus to drown out the siren song of consumerism. He's given missional moms his anchoring promise to hold us fast: "And behold, I am with you always, to the end of the age" (Matt. 28:20). Will we trust him more than we trust our stuff?

You may have seen antidotes for consumerism circulating around your community. Downsize, declutter, live simply, go minimalistic, and eat clean. Any of these techniques may be useful in your struggle against consumerism, but if they don't address the heart issue behind it, you will still feel hungry. And when you still feel hungry, you'll consume more and more—more and more minimalism, more and more clean eating, more and more fair trade. Do you see the irony? Unless the heart issue is addressed—that God designed you to consume his word—you'll never be full. The idol of consumerism is starving, and its worshipers are never satisfied. But women who worship Yahweh will live by his word, walk in his ways, and be filled with his Spirit.

Magazine spreads show glorious living spaces and hold out promises that the occupants of such a home embody everything seen in the picture. The promise to the consumer is this: "Do you feel that your life is cluttered and you have no peace? If your storage room looked like this, you'd be peaceful." And so on. But the Bible teaches something different about home. The remnant Israelites learned that their home was not their refuge. In our modern time, we need to know this too. We need to know that our home is not a projection of our image but a space in which we work to display the image of Christ. Home points to a peace that is beyond color schemes and adornments. It points to the fact that the Lord is our refuge. We find the *shalom* we seek in him. Your house is not your haven; Christ is. (We'll discuss this more in chapter 12, in the section "The Strategic New Creation Ministry of a Woman's Home.")

Filled with God's word, the siren songs of marketing and the images you see will not drown you. When Jesus calls a woman, he bids her come and die to herself. In that moment of rebirth, her soul is resurrected as "a new creation" (2 Cor. 5:17). The old creation in her is gone, and the new creation in her has come. She is taken out of Adam and placed in Christ. Christ gives her his indwelling Holy Spirit as a seal and signifies that he will return for her to consummate his resurrection work and raise her body glorified. That day is yet coming, but for now he starts with her heart. Her heart doesn't have to be consumed with stuff anymore. The power that stuff had in her heart is broken. She doesn't have to eat the lie that Adam and Eve ate, now that she has been regenerated by the last Adam, who is truth. Mothering women who feast on God's word show the world that they've learned the secret of contentment.

So let's be word-dependent moms. Let's consume God's word to the hilt and shake the gates of hell with faith. Satan cannot make us trust our stuff (or wish we had stuff to trust). The gnawing pain of wanting stuff cannot destroy us, because Christ crushed the idol of consumerism on his cross. We will suffer no lack when we trust him. Our children will suffer no lack when they trust him. Let's trust him to be our daily bread. Let's trust him to be our children and our disciples' daily bread. When we trust the Bread of Life in this way, we can be prepared for him to take us out into the world so we can start passing out loaves to others. Christ's mission to glorify himself is our mission, and he delights in freeing moms from idolatrous consumerism so we can show the world that he is enough.

God Designed Women to Share His *Shalom*

God created women to nurture life by spreading his fame throughout the whole earth. But we no longer live in the garden of Eden, which he designed as a "temple" of his presence among men and which they were to expand over the wilderness. That paradise was lost when Adam and Eve sought to blur the line between their creatureliness and God's divinity, desiring to become like God himself.

Now we live east of Eden, in the wilderness of the world that is dotted with tiny pockets of local churches filled with Christ followers, who are the temple of the Holy Spirit. Through the work of the Spirit, the kingdom of God *is* spreading. Harvest after harvest is being brought in all the time around the globe. The Bread of Life is satisfying our sisters in Christ, and he is being shared and passed on by women all over the world.

Through the great cosmic conflict at the cross, Jesus gives his followers his *shalom*, his peace that surpasses understanding. No gimmicks, no click baits, and no teasers to get you to buy. The cross speaks of our dignity and worth as human beings as well as of our shame as transgressors of God's law. At the cross we see Christ's subversive solution to the problem of our sin. The evil powers and principalities could not understand this; otherwise they would not have stood to see the Lord of glory crucified (1 Cor. 2:8). Through the cross, the grace and peace of God flow to us. When our modern ears hear the word *peace*, we think of the absence of conflict, but the Hebrew word *shalom* speaks to the presence of wholeness. All the nurturing work we do points to peace, whether it is the peace of a fever cooled down by a cold rag, a meal to calm a rumbling stomach, or a hug to calm an emotional storm.

It's all part of our design as nurturers created in God's image. The temporary peace our mothering brings is a picture of the permanent, uninterrupted peace we all crave. God designed his image bearers to nurture life by pointing to the fullness of the *shalom* that only he can give. His peace is what satisfies the emptiness that we try to fill with consuming things. The power of the world and its images are broken—we don't have to jump through those hoops anymore. In our hearts the hymns of the new heavens and the new earth drown out the crooning of this world, which is passing away. "To him who sits on the throne and to the Lamb be blessing and honor and glory and might forever and ever" (Rev. 5:13)! Word-filled moms who live out their various roles and callings in their homes, churches, and communities know and cherish this fact with their whole, happy hearts: Christ is all, and he is central.

8

Christ, the Redeemer
of Motherhood

Once upon a church potluck, my three-year-old was caught hovering around the doughnut table like a velociraptor stalking its prey. Before he went in for the kill, a friend of mine broke his concentration. She leaned down and said to him, "I don't know if you can have a doughnut yet. What does your mommy say?" He blurted out for everyone in earshot, "What my mommy says? My mommy says, 'Flush. The. Toilet!'"

Every Mother's Only Hope

We sound like broken records sometimes with the things we always say. I bet if people hung a voice recorder around your neck and played it back at the end of the day, they'd track some interesting patterns. What we always talk about reveals what is important to us. What we say and write reveals what we place our hope in. Our words are the overflow of what is going on in our hearts.

Yesterday, it must have sounded like my hope was in one of my friends. I talked about how I was waiting to hear back from her. I reread our latest email chain multiple times. I kept staring at my phone, and kept refreshing my inbox. My insecurities about how I interacted with her kept coming up in conversation with my husband. Should I have said something else? At a different time? Or in a different way? How did she understand our latest conversation about some really significant issues? I was not as engaged with my kids or their stream of questions. I played a round of Uno with them while the glowing screen of my phone lit up my face. The message to those around me was loud and clear. But if you turned on the voice recorder on the morning we pack our suitcases to leave the country, then you might think my biggest goal in life is to make sure the trash and the laundry are completely empty. I sounded like a [grumpy] broken record! What to do? The overflow of our hearts comes out through a variety of communications, verbal and nonverbal, all the time. Nurturing women have a lot of different messages overflowing at the same time too: "Brush your teeth . . . be careful with that . . . just have that hard conversation with him . . . knock on the door . . . read this first . . . check your homework . . . I love you . . . Jesus loves you."

No Other News

Being a disciple maker means that the gospel is our one, main message. We are most concerned with obeying, communicating, and living in the reality of the gospel. The gospel motivates the way we care about the suffering we see around us. Communicating the good news clearly and faithfully is our goal in evangelism. And the gospel drives us to dream big, creative dreams about how we can invite the world to worship together with us at the feet of Jesus for all eternity. Making disciples is the priority of missional motherhood.

The gospel is *the* good news of missional motherhood. No other news can compare. No health craze, no safety tips, no school curricula, no positive pregnancy test, no social club, no bargain purchase, and no ministry leader can deliver you from the gravest problem you have—your sin. Jesus Christ is the end of righteousness for all moms who believe, and his person and work is also the message we communicate.

How does that old hymn go? "For my child's pardon, this I see / Nothing but the fact that she earned the Respectfulness Award in her class? / For my child's cleansing this my plea / Nothing filthy like Cheetos has touched my son's lips." Of course not! We don't hold out worldly fake hope to our children. We hold out good news: the gospel.

> For my pardon, this I see,
> Nothing but the blood of Jesus;
> For my cleansing this my plea,
> Nothing but the blood of Jesus.[21]

The gospel is not good advice for moms; it is life-giving news. It is something we herald. It's an announcement. So in light of this fact, I have an announcement to make.

First the Bad News, Then the Good News

Houston, we have a problem. Hyderabad, we have a problem. Hanoi, we have a problem. *World*, we have a problem. God is utterly holy, and this is bad news for billions of sinners like us. We stand up straight before God's law because we think we measure up to it quite well, thank you very much. Or at least we measure better than that mother over there, right? If we're not standing tall and proud next to God's righteous law, then we're ignoring it while we create our own moral code to live by. But we can't even be consistent in our own man-made rules. No one can. We fail at every point. What we need is for someone to point out that our self-righteous efforts are futile because of *God*.

> But who can endure the day of his coming, and who can stand when he appears? For he is like a refiner's fire and like fullers' soap. (Mal. 3:2)

No question in the universe is more important. Who can stand when God appears? God is the ultimate reality with whom we must be reconciled. But as we saw in generation after generation of people in part 1, no one can stand. No, not one. What we need is divine mercy.

And God has shown us mercy. Before time began, before we ever sinned, the triune Godhead devised the plan for our redemption. This almighty love could not be thwarted by even the darkest kingdom, the heaviest of disgraceful chains, the vilest covering of shame, the most powerful inclination toward sin, the most indelible stain of guilt, and the most reprehensible enemy. This God could not only create life, but he could *resurrect* life. Through floods, through wars, through slavery, through water, through fire, and through captivity, this God would not be stopped. He would make his name famous in all the earth. He would set his covenant-making and -keeping love on his elect people. He would restore unworthy sinners to himself. Our souls, though all hell should endeavor to shake, he will never, no never (no never) forsake[22]:

> even as he chose us in him before the foundation of the world, that we should be holy and blameless before him (Eph. 1:4).

> Christ loved the church and gave himself up for her, that he might sanctify her, having cleansed her by the washing of water with the word, so that he might present the church to himself in splendor, without spot or wrinkle or any such thing, that she might be holy and without blemish. (Eph. 5:25–27)

> And you, who once were alienated and hostile in mind, doing evil deeds, he has now reconciled in his body of flesh by his death, in order to present you holy and blameless and above reproach before him, if indeed you continue in the faith, stable and steadfast, not shifting from the hope of the gospel that you heard, which has been proclaimed in all creation

under heaven, and of which I, Paul, became a minister. (Col. 1:21–23)

For God has not called us for impurity, but in holiness. (1 Thess. 4:7)

Malachi asked, "Who can endure the day of his coming? Who can stand in his presence when he appears?" We have an answer through Jesus Christ:

Now to him who is able to keep you from stumbling and to present you blameless before the presence of his glory with great joy, to the only God, our Savior, *through Jesus Christ our Lord*, be glory, majesty, dominion, and authority, before all time and now and forever. Amen. (Jude 24–25)

God is extending to us his mercy through his Son. Jesus died for sinners, and through our faith in him we can stand in God's presence justified. When we repent of our sin, believing this gospel, we have Christ to gain.

No amount of ignorance can absolve you, your children, your next-door neighbor, or your neighbor in the farthest reaches of the globe. No maternal glory, missional ministry, or nurturing accomplishment can bear the burden of cleansing your sin. We are all without excuse for our sin. If we are not blameless in God's presence, we will be consumed by his wrath. This is our eternal need, but our everyday needs confuse us. It feels like our biggest need is a car that runs better, or a child who obeys fully, or a friend we can confide in, or a husband who appreciates us, or a church that values our gifting, or a ministry that fulfills us, or a body we are proud of, or a bank account that doesn't worry us. Any one of those things may feel like the biggest, most pressing need we have. But they all pale in comparison to our need to stand in the presence of God, to whom all glory, majesty, dominion, and authority belong forever. We may feel justified or empowered before our friends if we follow our mom-made rules, but not before a holy God who requires that we be perfect *as he is perfect.* Our biggest problem: our sin (not somebody else's sin). The only solution: Christ.

Herein lies our redemption from our sin—the person and work of Jesus. Period.

Redeemed from True Failure

Do you feel like a failure? To call something a "mom fail" has become a popular Internet meme. Insofar as this trend helps other women to see that they are not alone in their struggles, I think this is a healthy idea. But as Christians who hold out hope in the gospel and deliverance from another world, we need to be careful with what we call "failure." The redemption we believe in is powerful, transforming, and eternal. It is no popular hashtag or cutesy saying.

At numerous points of the day, I feel that I want to be delivered out of things. I want to be delivered from having to find things to eat that are good for our health. I want to be delivered from concern over my kids' academic futures. I want to be delivered from the lengthy amount of time it takes to drive my children to school. I want to be delivered from the long afternoons and into a nap to recharge my batteries. I want to be delivered from feeling needy when I haven't been around my husband for a whole day (or twelve days, like when he travels). Things that are part of our design—our need for others in community, our physical limitations, being embodied in an "earthly tent," and our lack of knowledge— are not failures. We have no need to repent of those things, for this is the way God designed us. God has no need to repent of making us this way, because he reserves the right to create in whatever way his holy will desires. Moms don't need to be redeemed out of their God-given design. But here is another place where we have to "use our words" very carefully. We must be very, very hesitant to name something *sin.* If it is sin, it requires atonement.

But we often place worldly blunders on the same level as unholy sins. Jesus Christ has no need to shed his blood for a mother's need to depend on other women for fellowship. The eternal Son of God did not go to the cross and suffer crucifixion and the wrath of God to atone for a mom's inability to accomplish everything she wants to do in a day. The Lamb of God was not esteemed stricken, smitten by God, and afflicted for the sake of women who simply don't know everything there is to know about nutrition, or the Bible, or childhood development, or whatever. Before we call upon the great doctrine of justification by faith alone to redeem us out of our so-called calamity, or before we herald the massive truth that we are counted righteous in Christ by faith in him, we ought to consider the nature of our need.

If that neediness is owing to your sin, that vile rebellion against your Maker, then you repent. You see the blood of Christ cover your sin by faith and secure your forgiveness before a holy God. You see the righteousness of Christ credited to you so that you stand holy and blameless in God's sight. You say the same thing you teach your children to say when they are given a gift. In light of the forgiveness you obtain because of Christ, you say to God, "Thank you!" You glory in his grace. Jesus shattered the power of the course of this world you were trapped in; he redeemed your life from the pit to walk in newness of life; and by his sacrifice he broke the power of canceled sin in your life. Amen and amen.

But if your neediness is simply because you are a human being (i.e., not omniscient, not omnipresent, not omnipotent, *not God*), then you have reason to rejoice. You see the love of the second person of the Trinity to inhabit the same earthly frame as the one you have. You see the intentionality of the transcendent God who made you, a creature, to know him. You see how your neediness points you to Christ's sufficiency. You see the wisdom in God's design to make you depend on him for everything you need. You say the same thing you teach your children to say when they are given a gift. You say to God in light of your weakness and frailty, "Thank you!" And you glory in his grace.

The Beeline from Forgiveness to Mothering

We keep talking about nurturing life in the face of death. If, in this chapter, I don't draw a straight line from this concept back to our redemption again and again, then I'm afraid the phrase will start to lose meaning. So here's another beeline: because Jesus has redeemed us, we can nurture life in the face of death. Because our Savior has freed us from the bondage of sin, we can do what he can do—we can nurture life in the face of death.

The relationship between our good works and our redemption is one of cause and effect, but not in the way that other world religions work. So many of our neighbors hope that they are doing enough good to outweigh their bad. They live with a low-grade guilt over their lack of enthusiasm for the things their religions tell them they ought to be doing. There is no cross in their faith; only crossed fingers. We, however, have been delivered *not* because of anything we have done.

> May you be strengthened with all power, according to his glorious might, for all endurance and patience with joy, giving thanks to the Father, who has qualified you to share in the inheritance of the saints in light. He has delivered us from the domain of darkness and transferred us to the kingdom of his beloved Son, in whom we have redemption, the forgiveness of sins. (Col. 1:11–14)

Let's look more closely at that passage from Colossians 1. *Who* has qualified us? Do we qualify ourselves by our good works and sacrificial care for others? No, our Father has qualified us. He chose to reckon our faith in his Son as righteousness. Now, what has he qualified us to do? Have we been qualified to pay him back in weekly installments of penance, tithes, and church attendance until the end of the age? No, he has qualified us to share in the inheritance of the saints. There is no way we could repay such a gift. No number of orphans to adopt, no number of meals to bring, no number of children to have, no number of programs to organize, no number of mission trips to fundraise. We do not serve the Lord in order to obtain forgiveness, but we serve him with joy *because* we have been forgiven.

Redeemed from the Futile Pattern of Self-Sufficiency

The climax of human history, as we saw in the sweeping overview of the Old Testament, shows us that the pattern for our nurturing is established according to God's character and values. Every time the people of God attempted to do anything apart from him, they failed and incurred judgment. The first and only person who nurtured others perfectly was a man—Jesus. Every promise he bought for us was purchased on the cross. His cross-shaped nurturing is a powerful demonstration of God's tangible grace *through* our weaknesses and sufferings.

I think the question we face most often is: Do we, with glad hearts, glorify God for designing this cruciform pattern for our work in nurturing others? I mean, it's wonderful that Jesus, "for the joy that was set before him, endured the cross" (Heb. 12:2), but *me*? How can I gladly lay down my comfortable schedule in order to serve someone? How can I gladly lay down my body to carry someone else inside it for nine months? How can I gladly lay down my fears and insecurities, pick up a Bible, and disciple some women? How can I gladly lay down my coffee to do *anything*? The answer to those *how* questions is found in the cross. We follow Christ, who laid down his life in order to nurture our lives.

Serving others from a position of personal weakness is embarrassing for us prideful people. We like to be seen as sufficient. We enjoy admiring glances. We brush off compliments of, "Wow. How do you do it?" but we relish those words and play them back in our minds. Distinctly Christian mothering is done from a posture of weakness and dependence. We nurture life in the face of death by grace through faith in Jesus. The cross is everything to us—not a bonus prize or safety net. He has given us a cross-shaped, everyday ministry of mothering others, and he has redeemed us out of the futile ways that we used to mother. We don't mother in order to obtain forgiveness, but we mother out of our forgiven-ness. (Did I just make up a word there?) We are free from saving ourselves or pretending we are strong. We are free from mothering our children in certain ways in order to obtain approval from other women. Our children are free from the unfair burden of becoming our saviors or proving our worth. (And all God's children said, "Amen!") And the elect among the nations are free to see and savor the sufficiency of *Christ*, not the imperialism of the physically, economically, or socially privileged women.

Missional Motherhood Delivers Us from Our Seasonal Obsessive Disorder

The missional vision of motherhood helps correct our nearsighted mothering. It propels us to bank on the cruciform victory of Jesus and look forward to receiving future grace because of what he did.

That sounds like a wonderfully lofty idea of religious hopefulness, doesn't it? But *the* blessed hope—the appearing of the glory of our great God and Savior Jesus Christ (Titus 2:13)—is a hope more certain than your newborn taking her nap this afternoon, more reliable than your husband coming home on time, and more sturdy than your commitment to pray for your unbelieving friend. Christ's return is the future of this present age, which is passing away. His second advent will mark the commencement of the fullness of the new creation. You can bank on it. No, you *must* bank on it. You must look forward to it. You must hang onto that blessed hope. You will not be disappointed. We can't say so much for our other hopes, now, can we?

We like to encourage ourselves and each other with short-term encouragements such as, "Just hang in there; I promise you'll feel stronger in the second trimester." Or, "Once we get this or get rid of that, life in our home will be easier." Or, "After the kids reach a certain age, our family life will be more enjoyable." "This new Bible study or book will do the trick for my problems." And those thoughts may be of some help. But these temporary helps cannot compare to the hope we receive from considering the *real* long view.

The real long view is actually longer than we think. It wasn't at the end of the ark's voyage atop miles of water. It wasn't at the end of Sarah's barrenness. It wasn't at the end of the Hebrews' Egyptian slavery. It wasn't at the end of the conquest of Canaan. It wasn't at the dedication of the temple. It wasn't at the beginning of the exiles' return, temple construction, or wall restoration. The long view is not at the end of this no-good, terrible day. Or at the end of this magically brilliant day. It's not at the end of five years or seventy-five years. Or five hundred years. The long view stretches past whatever earthly ideas we have into a vision of a new world, into eternity and the new earth. Contrary to popular opinion, when we mothers take this long view, we actually become *so* heavenly minded that we are of *immense* earthly good today. If we want to get technical, we should say that the real long view is not actually even *heavenly* minded—it's *new-earthly minded*. We're looking forward to the consummated new creation. Being new-earthly minded corrects our Seasonal Obsessive Disorder. It corrects our nearsightedness and returns our vision to God's mission to glorify his name in all the earth.

You've probably heard of Seasonal Affective Disorder. It's a common condition among people who live close to the north or the south poles, where daylight is dramatically limited during certain times of the year. Sometimes SAD affects people who live in regions of the world that experience overcast and rainy weather. The locals describe feeling gloomy enough to match the ever-present, dark clouds in the sky. Well, Seasonal *Obsessive* Disorder is just something I made up to remind myself of the hope I have in Christ. SOD is a condition in which you are preoccupied with finding a name for your temporary circumstances. You define them, obsessively compare your circumstances to others, and covet a season that God has not given to you. I seasonally suffer from SOD and self-medicate with things such as coffee, complaining, and daydreaming. *When this is over, or this begins, or this changes, or we fix this—or whatever—then, I'll be content. Last day of school. Never mind,* first *day of school!* Does that sound familiar?

The missional vision of our motherhood, with its sights set on the return of Christ, reminds us that we are all currently in the season of *life*. We are all in this season, from empty nesters to singles to widows to new moms to high school students and every other woman. It's true of all of us. We get to live outside of the garden. We get to *live*.

Life in the Eternal "New Normal"

I need my shortsighted vision of motherhood corrected with an eternal perspective. Otherwise I will not keep my gaze fixed on the horizon of eternity. I will not believe (and live like I believe) that sin—my sin and my children's sin and my neighbors' sin—is our biggest problem. I will not hold out the gospel of Jesus Christ to myself or anyone else. I will ignore the deepest needs around me and pretend they are insignificant. I'll stare at my navel and wait for a new "season," neglecting the fact that right now and forever I am in a season of *life*.

God's gracious gift of life, in spite of our sin, is overwhelming. We are *alive* for a purpose—to make known the Lord's mighty deeds among the nations. Let your mind be blown by the reality that Jesus is currently, intentionally holding our very lives together by the word of his power. What mercy! Whatever season we are in, and whatever kind of nurturing work we are doing, and however long our season lasts, life in Christ is our new normal. And it will still be thirty trillion years from now. We are in a season of life in Christ forever! And this year. This month. Today. Right now. His grave is empty. Somewhere in Palestine there is a hole in a rock that once held a lifeless body for three days until Jesus, the resurrection and the life, walked out. The world hasn't been the same since. By the grace of God, you and I get to live in light of this cosmic renewal. *I can't even.* Isn't that what the cool kids say nowadays? Did I use that in the right context? I can't even begin to wrap my mind around that. We get to taste eternity now.

With God's promises of future grace strengthening our hearts and hands, we can enjoy an eternal perspective as we mother others. *In the middle of* the pain of life in a fallen world, we groan with hope, knowing that when the new creation does come in its fullness, then all our groaning will not be remembered. In light of the long view, they are just "former-world" problems. Because Christ burst through the de-creating cords of death and into eternal, resurrection life, suffering is not the end of our story. We can rejoice that the thousand deaths to self that we die each day are our servants—midwives that are bringing us *gain*, an eternal weight of glory. We nurture others in view of God's promise of future grace in Christ.

Jesus redeemed our motherhood from the futility of sin. We follow in Christ's pattern by laying down our lives. We serve with the power that he provides, and we look forward to the fruition of God's promises by faith. We live out his big story, the story that says:

> Therefore, if anyone is in Christ, he is a new creation. The old has passed away; behold, the new has come. (2 Cor. 5:17)

The old would not have passed away if Christ had not come. We nurture others as a new creation in Christ. That's our story. Let's live out of *that*. Our nurturing work done unto Christ is part and parcel of the new creation, an invisible kingdom that is growing like a mustard seed in a garden, and spreading throughout dough like leaven. It's the story that says:

> For by grace you have been saved through faith. And this is not your own doing; it is the gift of God, not a result of works, so that no one may boast. For we are his workmanship,

created in Christ Jesus for good works, which God prepared beforehand, that we should walk in them. (Eph. 2:8–10)

We go about the good work God has prepared for us, knowing that our salvation (and the salvation of those we care for) is a gift of God by grace through faith. We boast in Jesus Christ and point to him. *That's* our story. Let's live out of *that*. Missional motherhood looks away from our works to the work that Christ has already accomplished for us on the cross. We freely and gladly follow his cruciform pattern because we have already been forgiven. We look forward to the promises he has secured for us on the cross. And the triune God gets all the glory when women say, "I will most gladly spend and be spent for your souls" (2 Cor. 12:15), because it is God who works in us to spread his glory among all the nations.

9

Christ, Every Mother's Prophet

No wonder we have trust issues. Ever since the cosmic upheaval in the garden of Eden, when our first parents submitted to the Devil and rebelled against God, we have been plagued by doubts. Whom can we trust? The course of this world has inundated us with alternatives to trusting God. We're told that each of us has a story, and coupled with the postmodern nonsense that all truth is relative and we should follow our hearts, we get the idea that "what's true for you is true for you." If everyone has their own story, that is their personal rendition of truth and trustworthy hearts, so no one can claim to know *the* truth. Trust me. Trust yourself. Trust the experts. Trust no one. We don't know where the truth comes from. Or if truth even exists. If we're not sure that God has spoken (and that he defines truth), then what would compel us to go across the world, or into the living room, to tell someone about him? If we're not sure that God has defined truth, then what compels our missional motherhood?

The attack on truth is nothing new. In the kangaroo court that would make a mockery of truth, unlike anything the world had ever seen, the chief priests and the Sanhedrin brought false charges against Jesus. Jesus, truth personified, was accused of lying. But

Jesus remained silent. Finally the high priest demanded, "I adjure you by the living God, tell us if you are the Christ, the Son of God" (Matt. 26:63). This was quite a statement for the high priest of Israel to make to the Great High Priest of all God's people. The high priest invoked the truth "by the living God" from the High Priest who *is* the living God. The living God answered and was then condemned to death.

Later, the Sanhedrin taunted the true High Priest, saying, "Prophesy to us, you Christ! Who is it that struck you?" (Matt. 26:68). In their mockery, they fulfilled prophecy. And in Jesus's peaceful response, he fulfilled prophecy too. He had already spoken plenty. These are his own words, the word of the living God, spoken through his prophet Isaiah:

> I gave my back to those who strike,
>   and my cheeks to those who pull out the beard;
> I hid not my face
>   from disgrace and spitting. (Isa. 50:6)

> He was oppressed, and he was afflicted,
>   yet he opened not his mouth;
> like a lamb that is led to the slaughter,
>   and like a sheep that before its shearers is silent,
>   so he opened not his mouth. (Isa. 53:7)

Jesus was hated and accused of blasphemy, and the world hates and accuses his followers of the same thing now (John 15:18–25). The world does not seek our loyalty to the word of God, but instead to a godless society. However, we serve a different kingdom; we serve a different king. Missional moms serve as ambassadors of King Jesus, bringing his message of good news to a lost world.

Do We Hear? Do We See?

Truth comes from God, and the sum of God's word is truth. Every one of his righteous rules endures forever (Ps. 119:160). The chief priests and Sanhedrin believed this. But they did not believe that "the Word became flesh and dwelt among us, and we have seen his glory, glory as of the only Son from the Father, full of grace and truth" (John 1:14). Seeing Jesus's glory, they did not believe that Jesus was filled with *the* glory of the Lord (Ex. 40:34–35). Seeing Jesus's humanity, they failed to see that God had indeed come to tabernacle among men once again.

The chief priests affirmed that long ago, at many times and in many ways, God spoke to their fathers by the prophets. But they rejected the idea that in these last days God has spoken to us by his Son (Heb. 1:1–2). Hearing Jesus speak, they did not hear Jesus and failed to hear the word of the Lord spoken through his final prophet. If we lack confidence in Christ's fulfillment of prophecy, then we won't see or hear him either. When we are confident in Christ's righteousness, we will die to ourselves a thousand deaths a day as we serve others. Where can we go to build our confidence in Christ for the sake of our faith and for our resolve to witness to our kids and friends? We fly to the Christ, the living Word.

Christ claimed that he alone was the sum of God's truth, and heaven gave a thunderous "Amen!" When the stone was rolled away on Easter morning, it revealed more than an empty tomb: it also revealed God's approval of Christ. In God's approval, we can bury our trust issues forever and confidently speak the gospel message he entrusted to us.

And the truth is, we need the word of Christ now more than ever. As disciple makers and mothers, we hear the alternatives to truth all the time. We watch our friends and children believe lies and befriend idols. A friend of mine is drowning in debt, consumed by her quest for bargains she doesn't need. Another friend is fixated on her mirror, obsessed with perfecting her image. We hear stories of people groups immersed in lies all the way from the cradle to the grave. Prosperity preachers sell blessings. Witch doctors sell curses. Palm readers sell fortunes. Who will deliver us from the satanic lies that suck us into their black holes of death?

Jesus Christ stands against every lie we have ever been told or believed or spread. He is every mother's prophet.

Why We Care That Jesus Is Our Prophet

What does this really mean, that Jesus is our prophet? Why should we care?

The skepticism in our hearts is quelled by understanding our spiritual heritage. We have to dip back into the Old Testament to see why it is such a big deal that Jesus is our prophet. What is a prophet, exactly? The role of the prophet was to speak to the people for God, as Aaron spoke to Pharaoh for Moses (Ex. 4:15–16). Basically, the prophet is one who receives word directly from God (as Aaron did from Moses) and, without interpreting or adjusting, presents the word. The term *prophecy* can mean "forthtelling," but in the context of the Old Testament it usually referred to immediate future events for Israel, Judah, and the nations.[23] Many oracles (i.e., messages from God) are layered in the timing and nature of their fulfillment. I like to think of the prophets as Covenant Enforcers, even though that sounds like a superhero name. God gave the prophets messages to share with people concerning Yahweh's covenant. When the prophet prophesied, he was not to speculate; he had to declare God's very words.

Read the international news this week, and you get a flavor of the tumultuous days we live in. This week a gunman murdered thirty-eight people who were sunning themselves on a Tunisian beach at a luxury hotel. The United States Supreme Court legalized gay marriage in all fifty states. Islamic State jihadists exploded car bombs outside a Shia mosque in Kuwait and a military hospital in Yemen. We get cancer from our food, corruption from government, and inflation at the gas pump. What does God have to say to us in these crazy times? Is our situation unique?

Well, the days of the prophets were crazy times in Israel's history, too. From about 760 BC (beginning with Amos) to about 460 BC (ending with Malachi), the people of God suffered unprecedented political, social, and military chaos. First, civil war divided brothers and sisters. The people's apostasy festered on every high place like a boil oozing infected pus. They faced opposition from Assyria and Babylon, more formidable foes than the Canaanites ever were. The people were frightened, enslaved to sin, and confused. The children of Israel needed to hear from God. Our situations today are not so different.

Whom could they trust? There were hundreds of prophets in those days, including false prophets, but only sixteen prophets were chosen by God to speak oracles (messages from him) to be recorded in his word. Moses had said, "The LORD your God will raise up for you a prophet like me from among you, from your brothers—it is to him you shall listen" (Deut. 18:15). Where was this prophet? When would he come? It was a matter of eternal life and death to determine the difference between a false prophet and a true one. Whose oracles about life, health, prosperity, and safety should they believe? Whose oracles about death, disease, destruction, and deportation should they believe? What about us? Who speaks for God? Whom can *we* trust?

God warned the people about false prophets who "prophesy to you, filling you with vain hopes," who "speak visions of their own minds, not from the mouth of the LORD" (Jer. 23:16). Their message to men and women who despise God's word was, "It shall be well with you." To all who stubbornly follow their own heart, they said, "No disaster shall come upon you" (Jer. 23:17). That sounds eerily familiar, if you listen to the promises of politicians, the ramblings of spiritual gurus, and the presumptions of TV preachers who are piped in through thousands and thousands of satellite dishes that sit on top of slums from North Africa to Central America. The ancient warnings are for us today. All day long the world hands us opportunities and justifications to despise God's word and follow our own hearts. "Hear the word of the Lord," these false prophets declare, but in reality they want us to listen to the lies of the god of this age.

> For the time is coming when people will not endure sound teaching, but having itching ears they will accumulate for themselves teachers to suit their own passions, and will turn away from listening to the truth and wander off into myths. (2 Tim. 4:3–4)

Like a pair of sandpaper earmuffs, false-teacher collections tend to come in sets. If one ear is scratched by one false teacher, chances are another false teacher will scratch the other. We understand from the testimony of Scripture that women are especially targeted by these snakes who creep into households and capture weak women (2 Tim. 3:1–9). Nowadays, false teachers don't necessarily have to go door to door in a community to start dragging people and households under through their poisonous lies. Because of the advances we've made in technology, false teachers can creep into our homes through fiber-optic cables. We can be fed false teaching through the phones we keep in our back pocket. Discernment is critical for our spiritual health, and it's not about having a "critical" spirit. Spiritual discernment is a gift to the church. How can a mother tell if what she believes is a lie? How can she tell if she has collected teachers who suit her own passions, or if she is wandering off into myths? These are significant questions worth asking fellow believers; your husband, if you are married; and your church leaders. To make an enormous understatement, we care that Jesus is our prophet because *we need him.* We are desperate for truth because our eternal lives depend on it.

Jesus Speaks for God, Because He Is God

Our eyes just skim over subtitles like the one directly above, because they contain familiar words and are an uncontested truth in the church. But proclaim this truth at the community pool, at a family reunion, on a soapbox at the street corner, at a block party, or in your office lunchroom, and you'll see people take issue with it. How can we be so sure? We need to be certain that we have absolutely *zero* need to look for another prophet after Jesus.

The Son of God is the one who fulfills all the words he spoke through Isaiah in warning people of the consequences of their disobedient unbelief. He described himself, the suffering Servant who would pay for the sins of many. There are many places in Scripture where he talked about what his kingdom would look like:

- Jesus spoke through *Jeremiah* as he took up his covenant lawsuit against Judah for her idolatrous liaisons and communicated his grief over her refusal to repent. Jesus described the cosmic reaches of his judgment and coming salvation. And, oh, the pictures he painted of the new and better covenant he would make!
- Jesus uttered his words through his prophet *Ezekiel* with stunning depictions of what it would be like when God would make his dwelling place on earth once again. The Word himself spoke through his prophets of how despicable sin is and how God will surely punish sin. He said that escape from the just wrath of God is possible but only by his grace.
- Through *Daniel*, Jesus revealed himself as triumphant over everything evil in the world and under the world and not of this world. Nobody messes with the Ancient of Days.
- Jesus blasted his enemies in power plays such as the battle of the prophets of Baal versus Elijah in 1 Kings 18:20–40. All this was in answer to his prophet's prayer "that this people may know that you, O LORD, are God, and that you have turned their hearts back" (1 Kings 18:37). And it was so. "And when all the people saw it, they fell on their faces and said, 'The LORD, he is God; the LORD, he is God'" (1 Kings 18:39). Would that *all* the people might say, "Amen," and every nation throw away their idols and worship Jesus.

The Word who writes history is the one who calls us to repent of our sins, chop up our idols, come down from our high places, and abandon the world's deceitful schemes for life. Jesus calls us to trust the one who designed history according to his will and orchestrated every minute of the future. We know whose side we want to be on. "The wrong side of history" is a misnomer, for all of history is on Jesus's side. It's still *his* story.

This Is Happening Now

Every mother needs to know to the core of her being that Jesus Christ is the one to whom all the prophets pointed. Jesus is the prophesied Davidic king who rules the nations. Jesus has thrown down his enemies, and by his Spirit he is victoriously setting up his church—that magnificent, multicolored, panethnic "temple" on earth. The dwelling place of God is now in men and women by the Spirit. Jesus is the true Son—doing what neither Adam, nor Israel, nor David could do—faithfully living by every word that proceeds from the mouth of God. From every nation on the earth, Jesus is calling out for himself people to be "a chosen race, a royal priesthood, a holy nation, a people for his own possession" (1 Pet. 2:9). Jesus is taking people out of Adam and placing them in himself. Jesus is replacing stony hearts with hearts of flesh. Every day the day of the Lord gets closer, and that is no vain hope. Motherhood is a strategic ministry in the hands of the prophesied Son of Man.

We serve in a priestly role as we present to God through Christ our pleas for his elect sheep scattered among the nations. "O Lord, hear; O Lord, forgive. O Lord, pay attention and act. Delay not, for your own sake, O my God, because your city and your people are called by your name" (Dan. 9:19). We serve in a kingly role as we spread the light of the gospel throughout Satan's counter-kingdom of darkness, encouraging one another and building up one another (1 Thess. 5:1–11). And we serve in a prophetic role as we hear and obey the one true God who has revealed himself in his word, and speak truthfully about him and his activity in the world. Of particular import for us in view of our missional mothering is to hear and obey what God has revealed as his purposes for us as women. Our friends, subcultures, and governments have their own ideas about the image we are to display and how to play that out, but do they square with what the Creator has said in his word? Is it consistent with the way that Jesus Christ is conforming women into missional mothers who make disciples in all the nations?

Our prophetic role in the world flows from the fact that we are created in the image of God and re-created in the image of Christ. From housewives in Santa Clara to grandmothers in Nepal, cultures across the globe currently formulate their own ideas for what image women ought to represent. (Not to mention the changing ideas over *time*.) According to whatever image the culture envisions, women are assigned their corresponding "women's work." The rationale is this: women do what they do because that's what they are. Such reasoning may be correct, but if the image is wrong, then so is the role. Just think of pornography or celebrity voyeurism as examples of this. What is the perceived image of women in those schemes? What, then, is the role women play in bearing that image? Think of the images of mothers in your own culture. Who or what are they supposed to embody? What are the corresponding roles for moms to play?

Into the fray of swirling ideas, the Bible affirms the unchanging, creation-grounded truth that women are made in God's image. Women do what they do because that's what God made them to be. We image the Creator because that's who we are— imagers of God. The *imago Dei* necessarily involves God-given capacities and abilities, but it also involves God-ordained activity. Women actively show forth the image of their Creator through the exercise of their God-given function and God-given calling (or, in other words, their vocation). We can use the terms *vocation* and *mission* synonymously. Our Father has designed for us a function and called us to exercise it through fulfilling the mission he gave us. Working, ruling, speaking, serving, nurturing, leading, teaching, and building—all these abilities and more are gifts from

God as provision for the mission he gave us to make disciples of all nations.

Happening now, all over the world, women are being born again and transformed into the image of Christ as they behold the surpassing, permanent glory of his ministry (2 Cor. 3:16–18). This new birth is a prophetic word to the watching world. Through God's gospel, women are now being conformed to the image of his Son. Jesus is renewing missional moms not to the image of Eve before she fell but to something more glorious—his own image. Women who are in Christ do what they do because that's who Christ is re-creating them to be. Missional moms experience the transforming power of Jesus as he revives in them new abilities to work, rule, speak, serve, nurture, lead, teach, and build *according to his cruciform pattern, empowered by his Spirit, and for the sake of his glory in the world*. These are not Super Moms; these are missional mothers. I love how Susan Hunt said it in her book *Spiritual Mothering*:

> As a woman's growing desire to imitate God produces obedience to his Word, she develops mothering characteristics. Our femaleness gives us the capacity for mothering; our faith produces certain characteristics of mothering. Some characteristics we see from the Scriptures are strength, excellence, tenderness, generosity, desire to nurture, comfort, compassion, affection, protection, and sacrifice.[24]

The Word made flesh is Christ himself, and when his word dwells richly in his new creations, then the world sees his prophetic word at work even now.

What More Can He Say? And What Do We Say in Response?

Advice peddlers, "Discover Yourself" gurus, and Internet forums have nothing on Jesus. But how attractive are their words to us weak, needy, self-oriented people? I feel as though a particular hymn writer must have composed his hymn with me in mind. The famous hymn, "How Firm a Foundation," actually starts with a confrontational question, and the comforting answer is implied:

> How firm a foundation, ye saints of the Lord,
> Is laid for your faith in His excellent Word!
> What more can He say than to you He hath said,
> You, who unto Jesus for refuge have fled?[25]

Jesus is the excellent Word to whom mothers hold by faith. He is truth. But often we are not satisfied with what he has said about who we are, what we are to be doing, and what he is doing in the world. But what more can he say? Is there anything else Jesus could say that would settle it for us? Buried under daily schedules, crowded out by smartphone apps, and neglected despite good intentions, our devotion to God's Word collects dust. *Father, you gave us Jesus! Help our unbelief!* The Word of God wrote a story, and we're living in it. Let's participate with joy!

King Jesus is the architect of history, all of which is pointing forward to the kingdom he is setting up. He is still preparing all things to be summed up in himself, when the fulfillment of every prophesied word ever uttered through his prophets comes. Nurturing women look to Jesus as the one who both makes and fulfills all of God's promises. Jesus truthfully spoke of the patterns, types, and prophecies "in *all* the Scriptures the things concerning himself" (Luke 24:27). He is perfect, enough, and true. His word, therefore, is perfect, enough, and true. What kind of responses are demanded from all who hear the word of God and see the ancient prophecies fulfilled in Jesus? How should we respond to him who is God, both individually and corporately?

This kind of response to Christ is contentious to the world: we don't ask him to bless our will; we seek his will. We don't follow our heart, we follow his heart.[26] It flies in the face of our privacy-adoring autonomy. It means we do not make up our own minds to formulate the truth; we submit to his truth. I don't know about you, but I see tremendous comfort in this application. How many times throughout your days are you faced with hard choices, required to speak wise words into situations, and called upon to make sacrifices for the good of others? Here we see the beauty of the childlike faith to which Christ has called us to live by. Look at the admonition to us in Colossians 2:8:

> See to it that no one takes you captive by philosophy and empty deceit, according to human tradition, according to the elemental spirits of the world, and not according to Christ.

All our nurturing work is according to Christ. His word frees us from the captivity of futile thinking that is animated by evil principalities. We are *servants of Christ*, as Paul often put it, and that is what his word frees us to be.

Catching up over coffee, chatting at the bus stop, scrolling through social media, mingling in the fellowship hall, lecturing in the classroom, leading in the boardroom—all our words are to submit to the truth of the word of Christ. His truthfulness, then, is the crux of it all, because if his word is not truth, then we are most of all to be pitied and deserving of any persecution we receive from the world for repeating his words. But if Christ is true, then we fear no evil, for he is with us. As he said, "The word that is written in their Law must be fulfilled: 'They hated me without a cause'" (John 15:25; cf. Ps. 35:19; 69:4). And what is true of Jesus is true of his church. He was hated and rejected by the world, yes. And he was vindicated and glorified by the Father.

Missional moms are word-filled women. According to Christ's pattern and by his power, we take up our cross in our mothering. There is no "mommy martyrdom" in God's kingdom. Taking up our cross in mothering others means that we give even as we die to ourselves, not as masochists but *for the joy set before us*. That's how Jesus gave, as the preeminent "cheerful giver" who gives not reluctantly or under compulsion (2 Cor. 9:7). We're free in Christ to be who he is remaking us to be: women in his own image. Our actions are consistent with his design and not the designs of the Devil. All the good works we do are strategically angled at showing forth God's glory, not in showcasing the image of created things. Around the clock and around the world, the work we do in our missional mothering adorns the truth of God's gospel that we speak with our lips and write with our hands and text with our thumbs. We're sure his word is sure.

The Gospel Will Take You Places to Mother Others with the Gospel

Our certainty of the word of Christ is what compels us to leverage our "women's privilege" in social situations around the world where male ministers are not necessarily effective or welcome. I'm thinking of the *zenanas* in Indian villages, ladies' clubs and tea rooms in high society Arabia, and women-only sitting rooms in North Africa. Women missionaries may be the only people whom Jesus calls to serve him in these societies and situations.

I could tell you stories of Filipina maids who serve as indentured servants to families in unreached people groups. These brave women sing lullabies about Jesus to babies who are marked from birth to be servants of another god. There are stylists who blow dry the hair of women who scorn them, and they hope that one day they might tell them about the one who was scoffed at for them. Many young, single ladies in our church work in the local and global airline industries, spending hours with unreached people in the air and spending days in various cities where the gospel has not yet been widely shared. Midwives serving in the bush of Africa get to catch babies and save women's lives and teach women about the man who is the way, the truth, and the life. Remind me, if I ever meet you in person, to tell you the story about the woman obstetrician whose faithfulness to the gospel and her sacrificial love for a tribal people were the way God began to move in the heart of a king. Male and female classrooms are segregated in the majority of schools around the world. I would run out of word count here if I listed all the incredible testimonies I have heard from women who are teaching girls in gender-segregated classroom settings. The extraordinary grace of God is what compels these women to faithfully speak his word in these everyday scenarios.

This same certainty in the word of Christ keeps my friend serving in a region of the world where people suffer from boils and other skin diseases. One day, she started getting boils on her face. On. Her. Face. She looked in the mirror and saw scars on her previously smooth complexion. She wouldn't be scarred if she wasn't living sacrificially among that people group, but she knows that her Savior wouldn't be scarred either if he hadn't given his life as a sacrifice for hers. Now, you know you can't live somewhere or serve in some way and make any kind of sacrifice along the way unless you believe it is worth it. Is the word of God true? Does Jesus really want a witness in that place? Does he really want *her* family to be that witness? The scars of Jesus are beautiful to us, because we see his love in them. Her scars are beautiful to the disciples she is making because they see his love in them too. What kind of love counts a clear complexion and material comfort as *loss* for the sake of knowing Christ and bringing others along as you cross heaven's shore at the end of your appointed life?

These are just missional, mothering ambassadors of Jesus, leveraging their women's privilege for the sake of the gospel. Only Jesus knows how many more women he will call to serve him in this way. Perhaps you know of a "women's privilege" situation in your community. Is there a single mom on your street, a halfway house for abused teen girls in your community, or a pregnancy resource center in your city? The word of Christ compels us to get over ourselves and trek into villages, drive across town on a Saturday morning, or cross the playground to meet someone new. Beautiful feet shod with the gospel of peace are what take us step-by-step of the way. Romans 10:15 says,

And how are they to preach unless they are sent? As it is written, "How beautiful are the feet of those who preach the good news!"

In that verse, Paul is quoting from Isaiah 52, and the prophet is not talking about a Judean pedicure with Dead Sea salt. He's talking about something much more beautiful than our idea of pretty feet. Our beauty comes from what we carry—the gospel. Christ's certainty in the word compelled him to lay down his life for the sake of the sheep, and we follow our Shepherd and do the same in a thousand ways every day. Perhaps some of us will be called to give up our physical lives for the sake of the gospel.

As we are going and mothering disciples, would we rejoice, rejoice, for Immanuel—God with us—is here. His word assures us that he has been given authority over all things, and he is with us to the end of the age. His word will never pass away. Where is the gospel propelling your feet today?

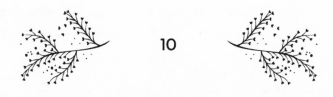

10

Christ, Every Mother's Priest

Every morning between 4:00 and 5:00 a.m., the call to prayer sounds off from the loudspeakers attached to the mosques in my neighborhood. If I'm already awake and sitting in the living room, I can hear it bounce off the cement walls of the downtown apartment complex where we live. I can hear my neighbor's heavy front door close and his sandaled footsteps shuffle down the hallway, keys clinking in his pocket. He answers the call to prayer and walks to the nearest mosque to undergo a cleansing ritual and pray.

In part 1, we saw how, in the Old Testament, God prescribed sacrifices for the people's sin, to be carried out by the priestly tribe of Levi. Those sacrifices were a pattern for a future sacrifice. After hundreds of years, and after hundreds of thousands of animals were slaughtered for the people, the last sacrifice for sins was made. We affirm what Scripture says about how "it is impossible for the blood of bulls and goats to take away sins" (Heb. 10:4). So what was the temple worship all about? It was a temporary shadow of something permanent.

We hear a lot about moms making sacrifices. We could count the cost of bearing children in monetary value, time spent, sleep lost, food consumed, and stretch marks earned. But the sacrifices of our missional motherhood cost someone his life. These fleeting, temporary sufferings we undergo for the sake of others were purchased not by us but ultimately by someone else. This chapter is about the person who paid the price for our priestly ministry.

The Picture Hezekiah Painted

In Exodus 19:6, the Lord set apart Israel to be a kingdom of priests and a holy nation. But they broke Yahweh's covenant, failed to make acceptable sacrifices to God, and defamed his name in the land God called them to rule. Generation after generation neglected this holy calling. Then one day, God raised up a king whose heart was disturbed by such gross, national pride.

Young King Hezekiah was aware of the Assyrian threat along the borders, but he knew something more terrible and threatening was inside his country: the people's arrogant neglect of God. In 2 Chronicles 30 we read that God's people had not been observing Passover, and the priests had not been keeping themselves set apart according to the way God had prescribed.

There was a remnant of faithful people in Jerusalem who wanted to celebrate Passover, and King Hezekiah sent couriers throughout the land to call people back to come celebrate with them. The text says that when the couriers went from city to city, the people "laughed them to scorn and mocked them" (v. 10). "No, we will not go to the house of the Lord for his Passover," was their answer. "However, some men of Asher, of Manasseh, and of Zebulun humbled themselves and came to Jerusalem" (v. 11). A faithful remnant of the people—the people who were "to be to me a kingdom of priests and a holy nation"—responded to the king's call to worship.

A verse later, we read that a majority of the people had not cleansed themselves for the feast, and they also ate the Passover meal in a way that was against God's instructions. One would expect some kind of divine retribution for this disregard, right? Well, the people had a kingly mediator:

> For Hezekiah had prayed for them, saying, "May the good
> LORD pardon everyone who sets his heart to seek God, the
> Lord, the God of his fathers, even though not according to the
> sanctuary's rules of cleanness." (vv. 18–19)

King Hezekiah played the part of a high priest, calling on the
Lord to forgive the sin of the people, and God answered affirma-
tively. "And the LORD heard Hezekiah and healed the people"
(v. 20). After they observed the Passover, the people went out
into the cities of Judah and cut down the idolatrous images they
had created and tore down the altars they had made to worship demons. Hezekiah the priest king reorganized the priests
and reestablished the proper worship of Yahweh throughout his
kingdom.

> Thus Hezekiah did throughout all Judah, and he did what was
> good and right and faithful before the LORD his God. And
> every work that he undertook in the service of the house of
> God and in accordance with the law and the commandments,
> seeking his God, he did with all his heart, and prospered.
> (2 Chron. 31:20–21)

Keep tracking with me. Through Hezekiah's contemporary, the
prophet Isaiah, the eternal Word spoke to this issue: "But you
shall be called the priests of the LORD; they shall speak of you as
the ministers of our God" (Isa. 61:6).

Christ's Melchizedekian Ministry to Moms

So, thousands of years later, what does this have to do with us? Or
motherhood? The connection is a direct line between God's plan
for all of his people to be priests unto him, *not* just those who are
biologically related to Levi by blood. By faith and through someone else's blood, we are related to a descendant of Judah, Jesus
Christ, and it is through Jesus that we have our priestly ministry.
Hezekiah's priestly intercession and kingly leadership are a picture

152 The Everyday Ministry of Motherhood

of what Jesus does for us. Our priest king Jesus cleanses us with his own blood of sacrifice for our sins. He sets us apart to be like living stones "being built up as a spiritual house, to be a holy priesthood, to offer spiritual sacrifices acceptable to God through Jesus Christ" (1 Pet. 2:5).

How does Jesus fulfill his prophecy in Isaiah 61? The clearest teaching we have in the New Testament on this subject is found in Hebrews 7 on the Melchizedekian priesthood of Jesus. (It's okay to admit it—the priestly order of Melchizedek is a little tricky to understand.) Who is Melchizedek? Why does Abraham give him a tithed tribute? What is the connection to Jesus? Does this do anything for my faith? How does Christ's Melchizedekian priesthood change the way I change diapers? What's the proper way to spell it in English?

These are honest questions. But they're not threatening questions, by any means. The Bible is prepared to answer them and strengthen your faith for motherhood through its teaching on the priesthood of Christ. Here are a few important questions to help ground your other questions about this doctrine: Jesus was from the kingly line of Judah, not the priestly line of Levi. How, then, can Jesus be a priest? Jesus broke rules in the temple. He drove out money changers and cleansed the outer court of the temple, and he healed people in the temple on the Sabbath. He did not approve of the way the Jews were regarding the place of worship God had ordained. What kind of priestly ministry, then, is Jesus officiating, if not in the proper temple at Jerusalem through the way people had been offering sacrifices for generations? How is Jesus different from all the priests who had been serving the people? We'll need to keep the big story in mind to examine these questions. In Hebrews 8, Jesus is actually called our high priest *and* exalted king. Check this out:

> Now the point in what we are saying is this: we have such a
> high priest, one who is seated at the right hand of the throne

of the Majesty in heaven, a minister in the holy places, in the true tent that the Lord set up, not man. (Heb. 8:1–2)

Even with just a quick glance over that brief summary, we can see that Christ's priesthood has a lot to do with our motherhood. Melchizedek points us to Jesus. *Jesus* is our High Priest, and he is our King. He has successfully fulfilled the priest king role that the first Adam and each of his children could never fulfill. That means Christ is enough.

The "enough problem" is a common one for moms all over the world. Even in my international context, I don't know how many times I have heard from other women (or told myself) that the reason we can sleep easy is that we know we're "just doing what we can." We soothe our maternal anxiety with the pacifier of our achievements. But at the end of the day, we're never quite sure that we are done with our mothering work in the sense that we have done "enough." Have we done enough to set up that child for success relationally or academically or dentally? (This morning a friend of mine told me she was anxious about her daughter's orthodontic issues: Have I done enough for her teeth?) Have we done enough to teach our disciples to walk in God's ways? Have we done enough to prove to others that we are enough (or more enough than they are)? Have we done enough to convince our fragile egos that we are enough in our own eyes?

We're inclined to justify ourselves to ourselves, and cover our shame from ourselves. And since there is no way we can truly justify our sin or adequately hide our shame, we stick to what we can do by a different measuring stick altogether. We trade in the divine standard of God's holiness for the world's standard of maternal accomplishments (defined and measured according to our culture). We saw in our overview of the Old Testament that not even the best of candidates for God's approval, from Adam and Eve to Noah to Abraham to David and Solomon—no one can meet God's standard of perfection.

The Priesthood of Jesus Is Better Than the
So-Called Prosperity Gospel for Moms

Satan knows our failures too. He knows we cannot redeem our-selves or atone for our own sin in any way. So to keep us from feeling the weight of the law, seeing the vileness of our sin, and then crying out to God for grace, he works to assure us that we do not need grace. We just need a boost. We just need a hand. We just need a second chance. We just need to turn over a new leaf. We just need a more attainable resolution or goal. We just need to love ourselves better.

These are deadly lies.

Satan has designed the course of this world and rigged it with false priests who peddle false assurance. Part of that despicable order is the so-called prosperity gospel, which tells moms that Jesus will give them super-knowledge for parenting, super-strength for serving, and super-abilities to fly circles around all the poor, lost moms. The charlatans crow, "All glory to Jesus who wants to be the wind beneath your Super Mom cape!"

Friends, don't buy it—it's a bunch of super-heretical baloney. We have a High Priest, who is seated at the right hand of the throne of the Majesty in heaven, a minister in the holy places, in the true tent that the Lord set up, not man. The so-called prosper-ity gospel would have you looking to God to "fix" your mater-nal weaknesses so that you overlook your deepest, most urgent need: atonement for your sin. It sure may look like you are being saved when you prosper materially and maternally. It may look like other women are being saved when they prosper financially, healthfully, or educationally. But Jesus is not a vending machine who gives you the stuff your heart desires. Jesus is your priest who gives you the atonement your soul needs. Run away as fast as you can from false teachers who want to sell you a god who exists for your maternal glory.

We can certainly give ourselves a high five for a job well done at the end of a great day, when all the loose ends are tied up and we have served our guts out. But we glory most of all in the fact that Jesus Christ made atonement for our sin, was exalted to the right hand of God, and sat down on the throne. Heavenly beings fall prostrate in the throne room of heaven, but the Son of Man sits down. Our High Priest is the exalted King of the cosmos. What mother wants to crown herself as "enough" when Christ is hers? Not us. We want Christ's power to be made perfect through us weak moms. So we will boast all the more gladly of our weaknesses, so that the power of Christ may rest upon us (2 Cor. 12:9). (Notice we boast in our *weaknesses*—not in our sin.) King Saul stood head and shoulders above the rest of Israel, but one thing he lacked—and it was his downfall. He did not have a heart for God. We may slump lower than the world in the things others esteem, such as power, privilege, fertility, and beauty, but our hearts are for God. Over and over again, the testimony of Scripture proves that even a heart for God is a gift of grace. The missional mother's credo is thus, "Not to us, O LORD, not to us, but to your name give glory, for the sake of your steadfast love and your faithfulness!" (Ps. 115:1).

Making Priestly, Motherly Sacrifices Because of Jesus

The point of Hebrews 7 is that we have a high priest who atones for our sin and makes our sacrifices acceptable to a holy God. Jesus has done, and is doing, what only he can do. His priesthood was not obtained through the "legal requirement concerning bodily descent, *but by the power of an indestructible life*" (Heb. 7:16). By virtue of his resurrection life, Jesus is our priest forever. He doesn't give moms a little boost to make it the rest of the way by ourselves, to the end of a long season or to the resolution of a strained relationship or to the completion of a difficult task or to the end of a painful labor. All nurturing work is done *through* Jesus, made holy and acceptable to God by virtue of the blood of the perfect Lamb of God.

When Mother's Day comes around (which is three times for

me here in the Middle East—once for Arabic Mother's Day, once for British Mothering Day, and once for American Mother's Day)—we hear about the sacrifices moms make. Even the world acknowledges that women make sacrifices for the good of others, and celebrates the virtue in this. *Amen*, I say! I appreciate the sweet notes and presents my children give me, and I admire the profound theological value when we honor someone who nurtures life in the face of death. (Just throw that out there next year to your nonbelieving friends when Mother's Day rolls around in your country!)

No matter the day, however, the priesthood of Jesus gives us a paradigm for how to think distinctly Christian thoughts about our motherly sacrifices. If we want our nurturing sacrifices and our motherly kingship over our domain to be accepted by a holy God, Jesus must be our High Priest. We dare not approach the presence of God uncovered by the blood of the Lamb. This is why Christian women have great cause for rejoicing—it's because women who are participating in the new creation through new birth are now, by the mercies of God, presenting their bodies as living sacrifices, holy and acceptable to God, which is their spiritual worship (Rom. 12:1). Through Jesus Christ our high priest, our good works are pleasing to our Father. He is pleased with his Son, and because of his Son's priestly ministry, he is so very pleased with us. Our Father confirmed Jesus's priestly ministry with an oath:

> The LORD has sworn and will not change his mind, "You are
> a priest forever after the order of Melchizedek." (Ps. 110:4;
> cf. Heb. 7:21)

Moms take confidence in the *more-than-enoughness* of Christ's sacrifice. Christ is the one who entered once for all into the holy places, not by means of the blood of goats and calves but by means of his own blood, thus securing for all who would trust in him an eternal redemption. His ministry to us isn't barely or merely enough, but it is a ministry of much more:

For if the blood of goats and bulls, and the sprinkling of defiled persons with the ashes of a heifer, sanctify for the purification of the flesh, how much more will the blood of Christ, who through the eternal Spirit offered himself without blemish to God, purify our conscience from dead works to serve the living God. (Heb. 9:13–14)

We have no need for "just in case" or "just doing what I can" doubts when it comes to our work done unto the Lord. God's confirmation of Christ's priesthood makes Jesus the guarantor of a better covenant. He holds his priesthood permanently, because he continues forever. So he is able to save to the uttermost those who draw near to God through him, since he always lives to make intercession for them (Heb. 7:22–25). Our eternity is secure in Jesus's nail-pierced hands, so every sacrifice we make in our mothering is *not* to strengthen him. It's to deepen our joy in his sufficient work.

Earlier this afternoon, I was a grumpy mom with grumpy children and well aware of the fact that we are all sinners. In God's kind mercy, he sent a few different people to our door to interrupt our sin spree against each other of rude words, grabby hands, and greedy hearts. But even before the knocks on the door, the Holy Spirit was beginning to help me understand how to make sense of all our sin.

I understand that I am beginning to participate in the resurrection life that Jesus has purchased for me by his blood. My awareness of my sinfulness (even in this mundane example of "What's the big deal?" type of sin) is accompanied not by an "Oh, well, I'll do better tonight" self-righteousness, but by an "O, Jesus, *you* do all things well" repentance. I agree with God's standard of perfect holiness and confess with my mouth, "I am not enough. Not even close. Forgive me." And I agree that the propitiation for my sins was undertaken by God himself when he put forward on the cross his one and only Son. "Yes, Father, only Christ can pay the debt I owe. I'm banking on him." I turn away from the sin that Jesus canceled on the cross when he offered for all time a single sacrifice for sins. Sin's power over me is broken. I can see that Jesus is sweeter than my sin. The siren song of sin is drowned out by Jesus's cry on the cross, "It is finished!" To see him on that cross helps me to see that even the forgiveness of my sins is not all about me. It is about the glory of Jesus, so that his name will be made known in all the earth. When he is lifted up, he will draw all people to himself (John 12:32). I see with eyes of faith that Jesus has taken his seat on the throne in heaven while his enemies are being made a footstool for his feet. By his single offering of his body on the cross, he has perfected for all time those who are being sanctified (Heb. 10:12–14). The rest of those who are being sanctified are still out there, waiting to see Christ lifted up. Who will show them? If your struggle with impatience is anything like mine, then you probably have regular opportunities to show your children in particular what it looks like for someone to glory in Christ's finished work on the cross as you confess your sin of impatience and repent of it right in front of them.

We all want to see the Lord and live, so we must "strive for peace with everyone, and for the holiness without which no one will see the Lord" (Heb. 12:14). The holiness God requires is in Christ, our High Priest. And Christ is ours! By his grace we work out our own salvation with fear and trembling, for it is God who works in us, both to will and to work for his good pleasure (Phil. 2:12–13). All the way to our home in the new heavens and new earth, our priest king leads us in this old earthly pilgrimage. Our priest king is pleased to work in us and through us as we serve our husband, kids, church, friends, and neighbors.

The Corporate, Missional Kingdom of Priests Reigning for Jesus

We say "we" a lot in the church, don't we? We call ourselves a plural people, because our Bible calls us a plural people. If the epistles in the New Testament were translated into Texan or another language that acknowledges the second-person plural pronoun, then "y'all" would be what we hear. Whether or not we have a copy of the Scriptures in those translations, we need to hear the "youz guys." We need to train our minds to think of ourselves as part of the people of God especially because of the influence of Western individualism in our cultures. Y'all, back when we were talking about Hezekiah and what he did for Israel in consecrating them for the Passover, we read in 1 Peter 2:5 that Jesus has made us to be a kingdom of priests. He did this to accomplish God's plan for his image bearers to be priests unto him. But to what end? In many world religions we see that priests are a mere spectacle or a ceremonial figurehead. What do we do as God's priests to the world? A few verses down we see the reason we've been set apart:

> But you are a chosen race, a royal priesthood, a holy nation, a people for his own possession, that you may proclaim the excellencies of him who called you out of darkness into his marvelous light. (1 Pet. 2:9)

Our sins had to be atoned for so that Jesus, our priest king, could make the church a kingdom and priests to our God so that we would reign on the new earth (Rev. 5:10). His priestly ministry to us is missional, and the priestly ministry he gave to us is missional too. We also see that he gave this ministry to us as a corporate group—as believers, we all, y'all, are a race, priesthood, nation, and people.

As I'm writing this book, the Islamic State (Daesh) is summoning all who identify with its evil ideology to come live in the land it has claimed as its own. The idea is this: to be faithful is to live where the faithful live. In the New Testament, we have an entirely different model for gathering together. In Hebrews 12:22–24 we see where all who identify with Jesus have come—not to any earthly country or political party or school or company or building—but to Jesus Christ himself.

> But you have come to Mount Zion and to the city of the living God, the heavenly Jerusalem, and to innumerable angels

in festal gathering, and to the assembly of the firstborn who are enrolled in heaven, and to God, the judge of all, and to the spirits of the righteous made perfect, and to Jesus, the mediator of a new covenant, and to the sprinkled blood that speaks a better word than the blood of Abel.

If you are in Christ, who is the firstborn from the dead, then you are numbered among the assembly of the firstborn. That's why we gather with a local body of believers—we have each gathered to Christ himself. When God raised you up with Christ he seated you with him in the heavenly places in Christ Jesus (Eph. 2:6). We understand that ultimately "the Jerusalem above . . . is our mother" (Gal. 4:26). To be faithful is to live in Christ, the faithful one, and follow him. Where is he going? He has gone outside the camp to mediate his new covenant and sprinkle his blood on the rest of the firstborn who are enrolled in heaven but not yet gathered to him. So where should we, the church, go? Y'all, we need to go to where he has gone:

> So Jesus also suffered outside the gate in order to sanctify the people through his own blood. Therefore let us go to him outside the camp and bear the reproach he endured. For here we have no lasting city, but we seek the city that is to come. Through him then let us continually offer up a sacrifice of praise to God, that is, the fruit of lips that acknowledge his name. Do not neglect to do good and to share what you have, for such sacrifices are pleasing to God. (Heb. 13:12–16)

Jesus invites his followers to join him outside the camp, scattered in his world, to spread his kingdom through suffering with him. Perhaps you've heard some prayers asking that God would "go before us" in our everyday ministry efforts. Friends, he has! Let's follow him. *Together*, let's go to the living room to nurture that child, to the woman in the office next door, to the other side of the cafeteria, to the party where people worship what they can see, to the refugees who eat at that lunch spot that serves their favorite dishes from home, and to the Sebuyau in Malaysia. Through Christ, then, let us continually offer up a sacrifice of praise to God among those people. Such sacrifices are pleasing to God.

When Missional Moms Get Together to Pray

Prayer has been the magnificent work of God's priests since he first set aside priests within his chosen nation Israel. We, as believing Jews and Gentiles, are now that holy nation because of the person and work of the Messiah. But the significance goes far deeper than first glance. Prayer is one of those things that we tend to assume. We receive a letter with prayer requests and think, "Oh, yes. Of course 'prayer.' But what can I *do*?" If that's a struggle for you, then I want to share some encouragement. Prayer is something that God has ordained and that his Holy Spirit, the third person of the Trinity who indwells believers, facilitates. It is natural to look at a ministry opportunity and ask, "Lord, but how?" It is *supernatural* to look at your everyday ministry and say, "Lord, with you all things are possible. Even now." Through Jesus we are priestly pray-ers.

We can't overemphasize the importance of prayer, because God commands his people to pray. Prayer is the means by which God has ordained his work to be done in the world. Just a few clicks around on the Joshua Project website or your Facebook newsfeed will illustrate to you that we have a massive work yet to be accomplished in the Great Commission. The discipleship of the nations is an impossible feat outside of the strength and power of God. But we don't roll over and quit when we recognize our weakness. Instead, we see tremendous opportunity for God to demonstrate his strength through weak vessels like us. And this drives us to prayer.

God is delighted to respond to our faith-filled, Spirit-led prayers, and he sends his resources for his ministry in abundance. John Calvin called prayer "the chief exercise of faith."[27] With eyes of faith we see that God is able. He is willing, and so we believe God and pray. The opposite, prayerlessness, is an expression of our lack of faith that God is able or willing. We've seen how the whole of Scripture testifies to the absolute sovereignty of God, and we hold that truth together with other truths such as, "You do not have, because you do not ask" (James 4:2). So we believe God, and we pray. We ask God to do things that can't be explained apart from his power executing his sovereign will. The disciples came up to Jesus and asked him, "Lord, teach us to multiply bread and fishes." No, they said, "Lord, teach us to pray." If we don't know what to ask for (and none of us really does), then we can open up his word and ask him to let his will be done on earth as it is done in heaven. To encourage one another to pray is not legalism; it is *breathing*.

Prayer is a reflex of seeing God's sovereignty. Listen to how Martyn Lloyd-Jones encourages preachers to pray. He's talking to preachers, but mothers also can be edified by his words:

> Always respond to every impulse to pray. . . . Where does it come from? It is the work of the Holy Spirit (Phil 2:12–13). This often leads to some of the most remarkable experiences in the life of the minister. So never resist, never postpone it, never push it aside because you are busy. Give yourself to it, yield to it; and you will find not only that you have not been wasting time with respect to the matter with which you are dealing but that actually it has helped you greatly in that respect. . . . Such a call to prayer must never be regarded as a distraction; always respond to it immediately, and thank God if it happens to you frequently.[28]

God so delights in the prayers of his people that he gives us many pictures by which we can understand it. Remember that in the tabernacle he prescribed an incense-burning altar (Ex. 30:1). And the psalmist asks God to accept his prayers as he accepts incense:

> Let my prayer be counted as incense before you,
>   and the lifting up of my hands as the evening sacrifice!
>   (Ps. 141:2)

Jesus is "the faithful witness, the firstborn of the dead, and the ruler of kings on earth" (Rev. 1:5). He is the one who loves us and has freed us from our sins by his blood and made us a kingdom, priests to his God and Father. And he is coming with the clouds! Every eye will see him, even those who pierced him, and all tribes of the earth will wail on account of him (vv. 6–7). The apocalyptic vision of Jesus seen by the apostle John, when he wrote those words to the churches, was one of tremendous theological significance. Jesus in his resurrection life in heaven is yet a man—and he is "clothed with a long robe and with a golden sash around his chest" (Rev. 1:13). Those are the garments of the high priest. This is Jesus Christ, our High Priest, whose sacrifice on the cross has atoned for our sin and whose blood purifies our living sacrifices to God.

Prayer is the privilege of missional motherhood. Pray for the global church, the church in your country, and the church in your city. Pray for yourself and your family. Pray regularly with other women and don't cut yourself off from God's blessing through corporate prayer. We pray because that's who God made us to be—priests unto him.

"Keep calm and pray" is more like, "Pray, and then step aside to watch the almighty God thunder forth his fire from heaven and shake the foundations of the earth." See what God will do with the pleas of praying moms all over the world from all of time:

> And another angel came and stood at the altar with a golden censer, and he was given much incense to offer with the prayers of all the saints on the golden altar before the throne, and the smoke of the incense, with the prayers of the saints, rose before God from the hand of the angel. Then the angel took the censer and filled it with fire from the altar and threw it on the earth, and there were peals of thunder, rumblings, flashes of lightning, and an earthquake. (Rev. 8:3–5; see also 5:8)

Today, missions is basically the fruit of prayer being picked up. And then one day when all the ordained prayers have been prayed,

God will bring about the end of time as we know it. His will shall be done on earth as it is in heaven.

Our corporate, missional, priestly motherhood is to everyone and in every place that Jesus sends us. Jesus is having mercy on your kids, for he put a priest in the next bedroom whose prayers ascend like incense before him as you boldly approach the throne of grace and plead for your children's souls. Jesus is having mercy on your neighbors and colleagues at work. He is having mercy on your neighborhood. The Lord's favor and his mercy are extending to more and more people all over the world, because he paid the price for our earthly priesthood.

11

Christ, Every Mother's King

Blind men screamed into the darkness as they followed Jesus, "Have mercy on us, Son of David" (Matt. 9:27). When Jesus withdrew from the crowds to the district of Tyre and Sidon, a Canaanite woman came running to him, crying, "Have mercy on me, O Lord, Son of David; my daughter is severely oppressed by a demon" (Matt. 15:22). Commoners ripped up palm branches and threw their jackets on the dirt road to welcome Jesus into Jerusalem, shouting, "Hosanna to the Son of David! Blessed is he who comes in the name of the Lord! Hosanna in the highest!" (Matt. 21:9). Little children clamored and squealed with joy in the temple, "Hosanna to the Son of David!" (Matt. 21:15). Mercy is here! Salvation has come! It's the plain and simple people who, plainly and simply, recognize the King.

Yes, Nathanael, something good did come out of Nazareth (John 1:46). He is Jesus, the true Nazarene (Num. 6:2), separate unto God and wholly committed to him in every way. And he is God, in whom "are wisdom and might; he has counsel and understanding" (Job 12:13). Jesus is the promised shoot from the stump of Jesse, the branch bearing fruit who is anointed by the Holy Spirit of wisdom, understanding, counsel, might, knowledge, and the fear of the Lord (Isa. 11:1–2).

And if the King is here, then the kingdom of God has come. After King Jesus rose from the dead, victorious over sin and death, he announced that he had been given "all authority in heaven and on earth" (Matt. 28:18). This message went out through his disciples from Jerusalem to Judea to Samaria and to the ends of the earth. Without exception, there is no nursery, no neighborhood, no train station, no doctor's office, no gender, and no tribe that is outside the reach of the Son of David's domain. Peter brought the gospel to the Italian centurion Cornelius, because "God shows no partiality," and shared with this soldier that "God anointed Jesus of Nazareth with the Holy Spirit and with power" (Acts 10:34, 38). Jesus is King of all the people everywhere in all times. Missional motherhood's calling and message are the same as Peter's:

> He commanded us to preach to the people and to testify that he is the one appointed by God to be judge of the living and the dead. To him all the prophets bear witness that everyone who believes in him receives forgiveness of sins through his name. (Acts 10:42–43)

As loyal subjects of the King, who is appointed to be judge of the living and the dead, how do we mother our children, disciple other women, and reach the nations? We want to be faithful subjects of our King because he is worthy to receive our worship. This chapter is about how Christ's kingship affects the way we view our calling as women who nurture life in the face of death.

Christ's Eternal Kingship Deals with Our Modern Mothering Issues

Eternity reminds us that our lives here are temporary. Missional motherhood is not just for women who have given birth through their bodies or for those who have adopted children born from the body of another. The motherhood to which every Christian woman is called is making disciples of all nations. We all must labor, prayerfully expectant that God will mercifully grant people new birth in Christ. Because Jesus is worthy to receive worship from the image bearers he has created, every human being is worthy of our labor and care in this endeavor of discipleship. In this sense there is no Christian woman who is child-free. We pass on the gospel to the next generation of worshipers, who will pass on the gospel to the next generation, and so on. The aim of our motherhood is to declare the good news to the next generation, "to a people yet unborn" (Ps. 22:31). We pass on the gospel because we know it is the only thing that will give our children the strength and motive to give their own lives in making disciples.

In theory, we affirm that this mission is worth our lives. But in real life, if you ask me if it is worth trading my luxurious comfort, then I hesitate. In these moments I'm not so sure that I agree with Paul that "to live is Christ, and to die is gain" (Phil. 1:21). But what if we mothers really did believe that—that any and every death to self in the cause of Christ is *gain*? How would it change the way we shepherd children and other women? Even though he was speaking to American Christians, David Platt's words are applicable to every believer who is tempted to live for the world:

> You and I stand on the porch of eternity. Both of us will soon stand before God to give an account for our stewardship of the time, the resources, the gifts, and ultimately the gospel he has entrusted to us. When that day comes, I am convinced we will not wish we had given more of ourselves to live the American dream.[29]

As we remember eternity and embrace death for Christ as gain, then our lives will change. One change I predict is that we will stop helicopter mothering ourselves and the people around us. To helicopter mother is to hover over others with the intent of controlling them and/or the circumstances surrounding them. You've probably heard the term "helicopter mom" in regard to how some moms tend to obsessively overparent their children. Child psychologists in the West have been documenting this as a social trend and publishing their opinion papers online. Sometimes grim forecasts are given for children who are parented in this manner: depression, anxiety, poor performance in school, and financial issues. In her article "Helicopter Parenting—It's Worse Than You Think," Hara Estroff Marano worried that with the rise of helicopter parents, "independence took a great leap backward."[30] She reasons that when we eliminate risks for our children, we will "rob kids of self-sufficiency." Marano, a psychologist, believes that the state of parenting is "worse than we think." No woman wants any of these things for her children or for the people she is nurturing.

I've heard Christian parents say that they loathe that trend, but we must recognize a problem that's *even* worse than the loss of independence that Marano and others bemoan. The greater concern about helicopter parenting is not that children will not learn independence, but that we will inadvertently model to them that God's faithfulness is not dependable. Because we've bought the story that the best things in life are health and youth, financial security, and self-confidence, which comes through subliminally in our helicoptering. In our mothering efforts we do everything "in our power" to get and keep those things for ourselves and our kids. The overarching consequence of obsessive overparenting is simply that in our failure to live out the truth of the big story, we fail to pass on that big story. What is this helicopter parenting subconsciously teaching our children about God, themselves, and his call to spread his glory to every corner of the earth? In our disciples' eyes it may seem that God, who is so big, so strong, and so mighty, is really no bigger than we are. God is not mighty to save; Mommy is.

Are we in danger of becoming so preoccupied with eliminating risks in our children's world that we neglect to encourage them to take risks for the gospel? For now, forget about the question of whether we let a child go down the twisty slide, eat a breakfast cereal with artificial coloring, or cross the street. Consider the noble quest of crossing cultures for the sake of the gospel. Are we parenting in such a way that our children will one day not hesitate to say, "I think Jesus is calling me to follow him into [fill in the blank: a hard place, a risky ministry, a university with less prestige for the sake of being close to a local church, etc.]?" Will we celebrate the kindness of God to lead our children to take risks and make sacrifices for his mission, to spread his glory over the face of the earth? Or will we respond with the common objection that many young people hear from their parents today: "What about everything that we have invested in you? Will you waste it?" We need to understand that our obsession with safety is not the gravest concern regarding helicopter parenting; risk intolerance is. When we spend unhealthy amounts of energy in training our children and disciples to be afraid, they will subconsciously adopt our anemic view of God. "If God is not for us, then we need to be for ourselves," is the mind-set. When we unhinge our obsession with safety, we can see that it is not held together by God's wisdom but by a demonic strategy to hinder God's mission. My friend Tim Keesee was speaking about the reign of terror and paranoia in Mao's China, but his words are poignant for this specific topic too: "Boundless terror is the greatest way to control the most people from the cradle to the grave."[31] Who is governing our mind-set about mothering? Is it King Jesus or an impostor?

If our stewardship goals are to get as much as we can of the American dream for ourselves and our children, then we betray our King and live as though his kingdom is worthless. I say those hard words just as strongly to myself—even now as my family is preparing to visit the United States for three weeks, and I can't stop thinking about chasing food, stores, and stuff. We need to continually renew our minds in God's word according to his story. Otherwise, we'll subconsciously buy into the helicopter narrative that gets its lift from the so-called prosperity gospel, which says we ought to have our best life now. Hundreds of Christian parents stand up in front of congregations every week and dedicate their children to the Lord. With great hope and expectations we affirm that children are a gift of the Lord. But, I wonder, what exactly is the nature of our investment? To which kingdom have we really dedicated our children?

The kingship of Jesus Christ and his authority over all things in heaven and on earth is sweet encouragement to this mother's heart. What I need to address first, then, is not the rules and cultural norms of mothering where I live. I need to have a renewed vision of *who* rules our family. I need to see Jesus. Is he worthy of our adoration when one or many of us are physically unhealthy? Is sharing his gospel worth staying in a place where we receive less than perfect health care? When I think of training my children, do I look first to bloggers or to the Bible? Is Jesus worth the sideways glances I will receive from the people around me when I parent my children in a way that honors him? Am I more concerned with the food that my children eat rather than what their souls consume? Do I point my children to worldly success as their big goal or to the mission of God as their reason for being? Do I believe that Jesus is willing to guard and guide our lives as we sojourn in this world filled with uncertainty and risk? Do I remind my children, by my words and actions, that God loves us enough to take care of all the "what ifs" in our future? Do my kids think I serve the almighty dollar or the Almighty God? Do we nurture our children with radical self-abandon, as though we are expecting deliverance from another world? Because we are.

The Kingship of Jesus Helps Us Get Real

Missional motherhood, in one sense, is truly radical. It's radical because the world doesn't believe Jesus is worthy of total allegiance. It's nice to tip your hat to him as a moral nice guy, but it is obscene to worship him with your whole life as though you are some "living sacrifice." It can also be said that this kind of whole-life, living-sacrifice mothering is *not* radical, because it simply corresponds with the reality of Christ's kingdom. Missional motherhood is our everyday ministry because of Easter. After Jesus was hung on a cross, offering himself as the perfect sacrifice once and for all for our sins, his disciples laid him in a borrowed tomb. On the third day life returned to his body. His lungs filled with air, his heart began to beat, and he opened his eyes. The stone was rolled away, and he walked out of that tomb. Jesus will never die again. He conquered sin, death, and Satan. His Father gave him all authority in heaven and on earth, without exception. That is reality.

Living in light of this reality is wonderfully, beautifully, peacefully "authentic" living. That is, it is in line with the truth. But because we still live in a sin-sick world, Jesus is still about his Father's work. Nothing is going to stop Jesus from doing what he came to do—bring all the prodigals home, rescue his lost sheep, and rule the cosmos with justice and usher in *shalom* unlike the world has ever seen. This Jesus is the one who stood on a mountaintop and told his bewildered disciples that they were to do the impossible, because he had the right to tell them to do it and he would be with them as they were doing it:

> And Jesus came and said to them, "All authority in heaven and on earth has been given to me. Go therefore and make disciples of all nations, baptizing them in the name of the Father and of the Son and of the Holy Spirit, teaching them to observe all that I have commanded you. And behold, I am with you always, to the end of the age." (Matt. 28:18–20; see also Mark 13:10; 14:9; Luke 22:44–49; John 20:21; Acts 1:8)

The Great Commission is what missional motherhood is about. Every time we look at our children and the ladies we are discipling and the neighbors who live across the street, we need to remember that all those who would believe in Jesus's name were chosen in him from before the foundations of the world. Making disciples of all nations is an expression of authentic faith in God. It's the antithesis to the course of this world that says motherhood is an optional venue for us to get what we can: make money, get stuff, enjoy stuff, and while you're at it, try to stay young and healthy as long as you can. We have the opportunity in our discipleship to teach our children and friends to discern the true story from the lies of the world. Not only is it an opportunity, but it is our job. If we won't work to disciple our kids, Satan will find someone who will. Part of a mother's responsibility is to help her children and disciples identify the cultural influences around them and the fleshly impulses inside them. We show them the better story—the real story. The song of redemption in Christ is more powerful than any siren song the world can stutter.

In our discipleship, which is anywhere and everywhere, from across the table at a library or on a dirt floor in a mud hut, we soak our disciples' imaginations in Scripture. In doing so, we can help ourselves and others live in light of the comforting truth that Jesus is the ascended and exalted King who is about his work of uniting all things in himself (Eph. 1:10). How do we do this? As we immerse ourselves in God's story, from beginning to end, we will begin to get a grip on what is real and what is not real. What is real, for example, is the fact that the gospel is God's power for salvation. "For I am not ashamed of the gospel, for it is the power of God for salvation to everyone who believes, to the Jew first and also to the Greek" (Rom. 1:16).

It goes to follow, then, that what is not real is the sneaking suspicion we all get sometimes that this whole Christianity thing is a sham and that everyone is "just fine" without Jesus. That is a lie from the pit of hell. We have no need to be ashamed of the truth. The gospel is God's chosen means for salvation. The gospel is the centerpiece of our relationships with our children, husband, disciples, neighbors, and strangers on the street. None of us is "just fine" apart from Christ. We're all needy, grace-dependent creatures whose deepest need is to behold our God and live to tell about it. The gospel is what meets this deepest need. We direct our conversations to serve the advance of the gospel in our dining rooms, cars, emails, pocketbooks, and everywhere else people are given the choice to serve a different king. The man whose voice is like the roar of many waters (Rev. 1:14) has commanded us to speak his gospel boldly and without fear. All of Scripture points to Jesus because the realization of all God's promises will come through him. It is a joyful thing to live in that reality.

King Jesus Ordains Every Mothering Moment for Such a Time as This

We have read in God's word, and in this book, that people are God's image bearers. Adam and Eve were given the royal task of filling the earth with more imagers of the one, true King (Gen. 1:26–28). Life after the fall is a gift of grace, never to be presumed or rejected, so we rejoice in God as he gives life to more and more image bearers (even the ones we humans deem as "accidents"). I remember when the sovereignty of God dawned on me during the nearly two years of trying to conceive our first child. When someone pointed out to me a simple fact of biology, that each fertilized egg is a human being, it just hit me. God had not ordained the child(ren) I imagined would be conceived during those months. Although I was still rightly grieved over the emptiness in my arms, I had a new peace in my heart. The same peace encouraged my heart when we did finally have a child, and I was assured that God had ordained this child (for he makes no mistakes and has no accidents). That peace strengthens my faith today when parenting my particular children is difficult. The minutes and days and years of all our lives have been numbered by a loving God who does all things well. King Jesus has ordained children and disciples and nurturers in his timing to bring himself glory in the way that he is so pleased to do. Therein lies a peace that surpasses all our earthly understanding.

Knowing what Scripture says about the kingship of Jesus sheds light on how we view our time. This is one idea that makes clear how the concept of stewardship lands right in the middle of the living room (and on the computer desk). Eternity seems so far away and intangible most of the time. (Unless you are ironing shirts, and then eternity feels very real.) Today, right now, because Jesus is King, we are to be obsessed with the all-consuming importance of seeking Christ's all-encompassing kingdom first. One great way to renew our minds to think this way is to remember that people have eternal souls. Of course, this fact is hotly contended in the public square, where in the West we are told that people have no souls and are just cells, and in the East we are told that people *are* souls (that may or may not have value). We interact with everyone, remembering, as C. S. Lewis said in his essay "The Weight of Glory," that "you have never talked to a mere mortal."[32]

Motherhood is missional because no mom has ever taught a mere mortal about how "hands are for helping and not hitting your sister." You've never wiped sweet potatoes off a mere mortal's face. You've never prayed for a mere mortal on the phone as you drive to work. You've never sat next to a mere mortal on an airplane. You've never received a bag of take-out food from the hands of a mere mortal. The fact of Christ's reign over all of these immortal souls means that our discipleship of the nations is an awe-full, serious *joy*. Immortality sounds like a subject that is just for mature Christians to discuss and debate, but according to Jesus we need *childlike* faith to live for eternity:

> Truly, I say to you, unless you turn and become like children, you will never enter the kingdom of heaven. (Matt. 18:3)

When we look at our children, the employee at the dry cleaner, and the person in the Internet stock photo to illustrate an article about sex-trafficking, we need to have the eyes of our heart fixed on forever, "knowing that he who raised the Lord Jesus will raise us also with Jesus and bring us with you into his presence" (2 Cor. 4:14). We want the sovereign Lord Jesus to grant these people mercy so that they will repent of their sin and trust him and therefore be raised to everlasting life and not everlasting torment in hell. So we pray toward that end. Your child is potentially not just your baby, but your brother or sister in the Lord. Think of it! Your daughter, a little sister. Your son, a little brother. When our children place their faith in Christ, they are adopted in Jesus as coheirs with us (Rom. 8:17). This is an identity that transcends earthly relationships. If there is such a thing as being "just a mom," then, sure, our purpose can be summed up in things such as potty training, working toward an illness-free childhood, or supporting children academically so they can be honor students or "make a difference in society" someday. But if salvation belongs to the Lord (Ps. 3:8), which it does, then our motherhood is missional. Evangelism is mom's work, but the giving of faith is God's.[33] We exist to point people to the King in all our mothering moments as we nurture life according to Christ's pattern and hold onto his promises.

The Return of the King

Each of us exists to bring glory to God. This includes each individual on the earth, our own children (born, unborn, yet to be conceived), and our neighbors (from the family in your house to the house next door to the house across the globe). We are all awaiting the day when the resurrected and ascended Lord Jesus Christ returns to judge and rule the universe. This day is coming whether or not we are aware of it. Our stewardship isn't merely a way for us to pass the time until Jesus comes back; it is preparation for what he has for us next in reigning with him (Luke 19:11–27).

We speak often of the return of the King, but millions and millions of people have not even heard of the first time he came. We tell the big story to our children:

> God created the world and everything in it, our first parents Adam and Eve sinned in the garden, and all humanity fell into sin and took down the whole creation with them; then God graciously gave Israel his law to reveal his holiness and set a little family apart as his chosen people. Then Israel failed to keep the law and rejected the Messiah whom God sent to rescue them. But, kids, listen! The mystery of the gospel has now

been revealed: God is calling all men and women from everywhere to repent of their sin and place their trust in his anointed
one, whose salvation is by his grace through faith. Now *we*
are in the middle of that story—a story that originated in the
triune God and is now being played out on the stage of history.
We are in *his* story. The loving command to repent of our sin
and love God with all our heart, soul, mind, and strength is
for each one of us. What will we do with our sin against God?
What will we do with his invitation to trust in Christ? What
will we do with our lives now that we know this?

Missional motherhood is a strategic ministry designed by God
to call people to worship the one who is seated on the throne
in heaven. The one who is seated on that throne is holy. John
described the vision he saw of God's throne as having "flashes
of lightning, and rumblings and peals of thunder, and before the
throne were burning seven torches of fire, which are the seven
spirits of God" (Rev. 4:5). God is receiving continuous praise even
from creatures of the like that none of us has ever seen, and day
and night they never cease to say,

> Holy, holy, holy, is the Lord God Almighty, who was and is
> and is to come! (Rev. 4:8)

We need to know that God's glory is being praised and will be
praised and that nothing will interrupt his praise. We get interrupted all the time. All the time! If you have young children in
your home or a phone in your pocket, then you know what it feels
like to be interrupted. But God is never interrupted. The worship
of Jesus is happening now in heaven, and in just a very short while,
we will meet him and throw our crowns down in front of him and
praise him, saying,

> Worthy are you, our Lord and God, to receive glory and honor
> and power, for you created all things, and by your will they
> existed and were created. (Rev. 4:11)

As much as I might want to hear my children praise my amazing motherhood skills, I want them to praise Jesus more. They need to praise Jesus—not us. They get a front-row seat to watch and participate in our family's goal to know nothing except Christ and him crucified (1 Cor. 2:2). Naturally, we want them to think their mommy and daddy are so great, but what they need to know at the very core of their being is that there is no one greater than the God whom we worship. We raise our children as we treasure our perfect Father (Matt. 5:48), who promises that he will keep us in perfect peace as our mind is stayed on him (Isa. 26:3). We affirm the truth in our words, yes. And we adorn the gospel by our reactions to the news, statistics, and nervous inner dialogues that go on in our minds. Jesus is worthy of it all. Since salvation belongs to the Lord (Ps. 3:8), we will relinquish our family to our King's competent and compassionate care and in light of his imminent return.

12

Christ, the Resurrection Life for Mothers

Jesus is able to give true life to all who call on his name in faith! And all the Christian women across the globe said, "Amen." But today is Thursday afternoon, and the kids are begging to go downstairs to the playground, but it's boiling hot outside, and we're currently in the middle of the month of Ramadan so we aren't allowed to drink water outside, so there's no point in melting at the playground. Plus Daddy is coming home soon, and he will want to spend some time with the kids while we figure out supper, and my contact lens feels abnormally itchy and dry so I should probably go get my eyes checked again, but I haven't got time this week. Oh! Grandma wants to Skype with us before we get on the plane to come see her tomorrow, and there's that grievous counseling situation we're dealing with that keeps coming to my mind, and I forgot to shift the washing to the dryer, but at least I finally remembered who is to receive the blank "thank you" note I set aside. What was that profoundly encouraging theological truth I was meditating on again?

Do you see why theologian Kevin Vanhoozer has likened

discipleship to the concept of waking up? Discipleship is like waking up to remember that we are alive in Christ over and over and over again a hundred times a day, until the day when we no longer need to be reminded that we are in Christ forever because *we can see him.*

Distractions are everywhere; you don't have to go looking for them. Distractions are osmotic, but discipleship is didactic. We need to learn Christ (Eph. 4:20). As we go and mother disciples, we need to be learners ourselves. Perhaps one of the most gripping and motivating realities of our faith is that when we trust Christ, God places us *in* Christ. Being in Christ is the new normal now and forever. The resurrection life that we see realized in our resurrected Savior is ours now in tiny tastes. If you've ever gone to an ice cream shop and forgotten what a particular ice cream flavor tastes like (or *pretended* to forget, not that I know anything about that, but I've heard), then you've likely received a teeny tiny spoon with about three grams of ice cream on it "just to see" if you're interested in buying more. Think of the content in this chapter like a teeny tiny spoon to help you remember what it tastes like to be a new creation in Christ. The texts in their larger contexts (i.e., the whole Bible) will prove to be much bigger spoons and even a backhoe loader (my son just told me that's the real name for the strongest digger in the construction yard).

Hold onto your spoons, and we'll dive into some delicious passages that radically alter the way we mother others in light of the resurrection.

What on Earth Am I Waiting For?

I always experience a dose of culture shock when I see commercials on TV during visits to the United States. There are commercials designed to persuade children to live out a consumeristic ideology, and commercials aimed at encouraging poor people to spend more money through financing gimmicks. There are even commercials that present the average person as a medical diagnostician and an authority on prescription drugs. "Think about it. You're probably sick. So many people have these symptoms and go untreated. You need to make an appointment right now to ask your doctor if Fancy, Promising Drug is for you," commercials suggest. This fits well with our personal story about being the master of our own fate. Or, as Nacho Libre put it, "I am the gatekeeper of my own destiny." At the risk of sounding like Nacho, to have control is to have the power, and to have the power is to have the prerogative for personal peace. I've seen this in my own life as I try to fix problems in my kids' lives and in the lives of people around me. If I have enough power, then I can solve problems and usher in peace. But the Bible says God has placed me in a better story.

God's word affirms that life and death are in Jesus's competent, authoritative, loving hands. Jesus is the author of life (Acts 3:15). In his earthly ministry, Jesus raised the dead to demonstrate to us his power over life and death. Then Jesus himself was raised from the dead. The ascended and exalted Christ told John that he had died, "and behold I am alive forevermore, and I have the keys of Death and Hades" (Rev. 1:18). Someday Jesus will unlock Death and Hades and command them to give up their dead in order for him to render his just judgments. All who have looked to the Lamb for life will live with him in glory forever, and all who have despised his witness will be punished in eternal, conscious torment.

> Truly, truly, I say to you, an hour is coming, and is now here, when the dead will hear the voice of the Son of God, and those who hear will live. For as the Father has life in himself, so he has granted the Son also to have life in himself. And he has given him authority to execute judgment, because he is the Son of Man. Do not marvel at this, for an hour is coming when all who are in the tombs will hear his voice and come out, those who have done good to the resurrection of life, and those who have done evil to the resurrection of judgment. (John 5:25–29)

The now-ness of Christ's authority drives the urgency of our missional motherhood. He is the master of all our destinies. Remembering that Jesus is the Son of God and the Son of Man who has authority over every person who ever lived is of primary import in our daily lives. You, dear reader, are subject to him. So are your children. You may call your kids to follow you and obey Mommy's instructions, but ultimately your children must follow Christ, repent of their sin, die to their flesh, and take up their own cross. Life and death are also his servants. Even now, while we yet live in a fallen world, those who trust this Christ are spiritually raised from the dead already though their bodies decay and eventually die. Do we mother like we are alive to Christ and happily answer to him? Or do we mother like we have no resurrection hope because we answer to the world?

We also need to remember that eventually we will be given new bodies. In the Gospels, when Jesus presents himself to many people after his resurrection from the dead and before his ascension back into the unseen heavenly dimension, we get to catch a glimpse of what our new creation bodies will be like. The new age interrupted this old age for those forty days, and things haven't been the same since. Jesus is now about his work of fulfilling the triumphant prophecy regarding the Davidic king:

> The LORD says to my Lord:
>   "Sit at my right hand,
> until I make your enemies your footstool." (Ps. 110:1)

Jesus will take care of subduing his enemies; we are assured of this in Scripture. Missionary David Sitton likes to talk about "purpose driven death," saying, "Has the thought ever occurred to you that God loves you and has a wonderful plan for your death?"[34] Now that's startling. It's startling because we look for life right here and right now. We want the best home now, the best health now, the best reputation now, and the best bank account now. We want a prosperous life now because we're not confident that the next life will be our best life. And we're scared. "All I want is a healthy baby." "All I want is *not* another baby." "This house makes me so happy." "I'm chasing my dream of being a ___." Friends and fellow mothering women, because King Jesus is on his throne, subduing all his enemies and supplying everything we need for life and godliness as we go about the mission he gave us, we truly have no need to fear. We can instead gladly embrace weakness, sickness, lots of children, a few children, lots of needy people in our lives, unemployment, financial strain, and pain, knowing that he is up to way more and way better things than we can imagine. We can do things that we think are less fulfilling to us, such as volunteer in the church nursery, simply because that's what the church needs and because Jesus equipped us to serve him and build up his body. (I use the nursery as an example because it keeps coming up as an issue: "I would serve the church, but there's no place for 'my gifts.' They just need help in the nursery and that's not 'my thing.'") Because Jesus is coming back, and he is giving us tastes of his resurrection life now, we can serve like he served in the contexts he sends us. We can go places we can't imagine will ever make us happy, because we don't need those places to make us happy. Jesus makes us happy. There is no place we could sojourn in our Father's world where he who says he is the resurrection and the life cannot satisfy us according to his word.

Back to 4:37 p.m., Thursday afternoon. I've got way better news than any click-bait Internet money-beauty-sexy-foodie-domestic-bliss gimmick ever attempted to promise. Jesus offers me a better life than I could dream up on my own through a smartphone photo fixed up with some cropping and a Valencia filter. There is no more beautiful, satisfying ending to any story ever written than "happily ever after," and God has written me into the ultimate story. Consider these profoundly happily-ever-afters:

> And this is the will of him who sent me, that I should lose nothing of all that he has given me, but raise it up on the last

day. For this is the will of my Father, that everyone who looks
on the Son and believes in him should have eternal life, and I
will raise him up on the last day. (John 6:39–40)

No one can come to me unless the Father who sent me draws
him. And I will raise him up on the last day. (John 6:44)

Whoever feeds on my flesh and drinks my blood has eternal
life, and I will raise him up on the last day. (John 6:54)

We have been given one life in this body to take up our cross every
day. One life in this fallen world where we can spend our days
and nights nurturing life in the face of death. We live and die to
be raised up by Christ on the last day.

The Bible points us to the true happy ending, and, furthermore,
it tells us that this is actually the new beginning. All those so-
called sequels and spin-offs are always lacking, aren't they? We're
looking forward to the resurrection, when we will receive newly
created bodies so we can be part of the consummated, eternal,
new-creation cosmos. At the end of his story, Jesus describes to
us all the things that will happen as he dissolves the old cosmos
and brings to fruition the new-creation cosmos that is beyond our
wildest imagination. Sufficient for the day is its own trouble, as
he said (Matt. 6:34). That's one tiny-spoon example of how resurrection hope just outshines any illusion of control I have over *my*
schedule, over *my* day with *my* kids while I live *my* life. I want to
seek first the kingdom of God and his righteousness. *Where will
you send your daughters today, Jesus?*

To live in light of Christ's resurrection is to be so heavenly
minded that we are of immense earthly good. When I encourage
women that nobody is "just a mom," there is one passage I point
out more than any other:

If then you have been raised with Christ, seek the things that
are above, where Christ is, seated at the right hand of God. Set
your minds on things that are above, not on things that are on

earth. For you have died, and your life is hidden with Christ in God. When Christ who is your life appears, then you also will appear with him in glory. (Col. 3:1–4)

Sister, we have died, and our lives are hidden with Christ in God. We are not our own. Our children are not our own. Our homes are not our own. Our stuff is not our own. Nothing is our own. It's all his and for his glory. And that's the incredible reality we get to wake up to every day. Let's help each other remember!

The Strategic New Creation Ministry of a Woman's Home

Most of us wake up every day in our own homes. The home, as we see in Titus 2, is actually not an accessory to display our unique personalities (contrary to popular Western opinions). It is a strategic everyday ministry designed by God to adorn his gospel in this age where the new creation has broken in to the old age. Our homemaking, when done in view of the cosmic ramifications of the resurrection of Jesus, is a ministry that can shake the gates of hell.

The classic text that we turn to is Titus 2. I realize that when some readers hear the term "Titus 2," they hear their subculture's standards for the home and feel discouraged. Baggage from our subculture's interpretations can weigh heavy on a missional mom who wants to please the Lord but can't measure up to the worldly standards that exist even in the church. Still, there are others of us who hear "Titus 2" and are encouraged, because we see that we are free. We're free to throw ourselves into the noble, Great Commission work of training up younger women and prioritizing the ministry in our home. We hear an exhortation to remember Titus 2, and it just makes sense, according to everything we know about the Lord and his will for our lives until he returns. We see this as license and liberty to go find creative ways to not compromise our core commitment to nurturing those in our home. Our ministry is manifold. We labor to support our husband in his work and ministry, and we see our missional motherhood as one-on-one (or one-on-___!) discipleship in training up our children in God's ways. We manage our home to be in line with God's truth to facilitate gospel ministry. And whatever else God has called us to do, we do it all for the building up of the body of Christ.

Context is king especially when it comes to understanding Scripture. Titus 2 is no exception. When Paul wrote this letter, here is what the people were dealing with. Rome was supposedly the eternal city. Word on the newly paved streets was that Rome was ever-expanding, growing in power, honor, and wealth. Does that sound familiar? No one wanted to be on the "wrong side of history" and oppose Rome. Rome was, after all, offering people a new era of history. But we know that Easter changed everything. When Jesus died and was resurrected, he inaugurated a new age that fractured the old one so that the present form of this world is now passing away (1 Cor. 7:31). This is the reality Paul is writing about. We live in a post-Easter world in which we get to manage little gospel outposts for spreading the good news. The sovereign Lord Jesus is ascended, exalted, and reigning. His kingdom is coming, and it is the antitype of the city of man.

Paul wrote about how this life is temporary and fleeting and that we were saved in hope of eternal life. We are coheirs. As easy as it is to get sucked back into the course of this world or discouraged by the mundane of everyday life, we need to keep our focus on things that are unseen. We need to keep those things in mind as we look at the things in Titus 2. It seems at the outset as though Paul is exhorting women to concern themselves only with things that are seen, such as husbands, children, and homes, but we need to remember that there is something unseen and spiritually powerful going on as we prioritize those ministries. It's resurrection life.

Just consider the issues of the nonbelieving Cretans in Titus 1:10–16. Many were "insubordinate, empty talkers and deceivers" who were "upsetting whole families by teaching for shameful gain" (vv. 10–11). According to one of their own prophets,

"Cretans are always liars, evil beasts, lazy gluttons" (v. 12). And Paul agreed (v. 13)! He explained to Pastor Titus that these wicked people claimed to know God but denied God by their works; in fact, they were "unfit for *any* good work" (v. 16).

But God, in his great mercy, saved some Cretans out of this mess of depraved humanity. So now this community of ransomed sinners ought to live as new creations in Christ, which they are. That's the basis for Pastor Titus's ministry to them in his teaching. Paul says to Titus, "But as for you, teach what accords with sound doctrine" (Titus 2:1). What is about to follow in the rest of Paul's instructions are expressions of authenticity as new creations. The Cretan believers have undergone a night-and-day transformation. Their dead souls have been raised to life. Whatever benefit we receive from the practical things Paul is about to list out here, what we need to know most of all is that it is "what accords with sound doctrine." That doctrine is the gospel—the word of Christ. It's the will of God. These are commands for God's glory and our good from the one who created us and knows what's best for us and knows how he will be best magnified in his image bearers.

So, here's what it looks like for the Cretan church (and you and me) to be pleasing to the Lord, obedient, and fit for every good work:

> Older men are to be sober-minded, dignified, self-controlled, sound in faith, in love, and in steadfastness. Older women likewise are to be reverent in behavior, not slanderers or slaves to much wine. They are to teach what is good, and so train the young women to love their husbands and children, to be self-controlled, pure, working at home, kind, and submissive to their own husbands, *that the word of God may not be reviled.* (Titus 2:2–5)

Reviled? I don't know about you, but I don't typically use that word in my everyday vocabulary. We need some more context for this term. There is another passage in the New Testament that makes the connection between home managing and the Enemy's slander of the gospel. In 1 Timothy 5:3–14 Paul gives instruction on how the church ought to take care of widows and which widows the church ought to take care of. In the course of his instructions he mentions younger widows and warns that "they learn to be idlers, going about from house to house, and not only idlers, but also gossips and busybodies, saying what they should not. So I would have younger widows marry, bear children, manage their households, and give the adversary no occasion for slander" (vv. 13–14). Paul's exhortation to Pastor Timothy was that he counsel the younger widows to marry again, raise families, and manage their homes, because Satan was ready and willing to give them a different calling.

Heading back to Titus 2, we look again in the second part of verse 10. There's the stated reason for the Cretans' new code of conduct, "so that in everything they may adorn the doctrine of God our Savior." In our everyday lives is where Christ's lordship over the world and his ongoing activity in the world come to light. Jesus said in Acts 1:8 that we will be his witnesses from Judea, to Samaria, to the outermost parts of the earth. This witnessing is not just happening when we open our mouths to intentionally convey the gospel message to a nonbeliever. Our witnessing to Christ's lordship and ministry happens even as we "adorn" the truth by what we do and refrain from doing. When older women teach younger women to love their husbands and children and manage their homes with Christ's lordship in view, they are acting in line with the reality of the new creation in Christ. When our actions line up with God's word, his truth is adorned instead of being reviled by a contradictory lifestyle.

The "good works" theme comes up a lot in Paul's letter to Titus. The term occurs thirteen times in the New Testament, and one-third of those instances are in Titus:

- Show yourself in all respects to be a model of good works, and in your teaching show integrity, dignity (2:7).

- Jesus . . . who gave himself for us to redeem us from all lawlessness and to purify for himself a people for his own possession who are zealous for good works (2:13–14).
- The saying is trustworthy, and I want you to insist on these things, so that those who have believed in God may be careful to devote themselves to good works. These things are excellent and profitable for people (3:8).
- And let our people learn to devote themselves to good works, so as to help cases of urgent need, and not be un-fruitful (3:14).

If we are saved by grace through faith, why are good works such a big deal here? The potential for God's word to be reviled is at stake if we don't make our words and actions line up with the gospel we have believed. Since we certainly don't want our conduct to be an occasion for Satan's slander of Christ, how can we become fit for every good work? It is fitting that we adorn the doctrine of God by consuming, loving, obeying, and teaching the word of God:

All Scripture is breathed out by God and profitable for teaching, for reproof, for correction, and for training in righteousness, that the man of God may be complete, equipped for every good work. (2 Tim. 3:16–17)

You can use the best homemaking techniques to clean your house, but it's just going to get dirty again. It's easy to feel frustrated about this (I have four kids—I know!). But it is the word of God that does the work of God in our hearts, leading to spiritual fruit that lasts until eternity.

Lest we feel discouraged by the hard-core, radical, new-creation imperatives in this chapter in Titus, we need to remember the gospel. Paul knew that too; just look at what's next in Titus 2:

For the grace of God has appeared, bringing salvation for all people, training us to renounce ungodliness and worldly

> passions, and to live self-controlled, upright, and godly lives in
> the present age, waiting for our blessed hope, the appearing of
> the glory of our great God and Savior Jesus Christ, who gave
> himself for us to redeem us from all lawlessness and to purify
> for himself a people for his own possession who are zealous
> for good works. (Titus 2:11–14)

Can you feel the focus of our missional motherhood zoom in and
out with cosmic, grand implications because of Christ's death and
resurrection? Jesus Christ is the greatest missional home manager
the world has ever seen. He builds his house, and he sets his house
in order. He is head over his church, and he loves her perfectly. He
nourishes her with his word. Christ reigns in sovereign superior-
ity; he is the basis of all our joy. We must live our lives focused on
his sovereign lordship over the cosmos. We bear fruit of his Spirit,
living self-controlled, upright, and godly lives now as we wait for
his appearing; he is our blessed hope.

So does bringing our home under the lordship of Christ and
waiting for his return mean that our house must be pristine clean
all the time? I don't think so, and I sure hope not. I moved aside
a pile of unfolded laundry so I could sit in this chair to type. Does
Titus 2 answer the question, "Can women hold jobs outside their
homes?" There are some who think so, but this is missing the
forest for the trees. The question Titus raises that we should be
asking ourselves is this: "How can we as Christian women work
in such a way that the holiness and hope of God is evident in our
lives?" Titus 2 is not about how Christian women need to be do-
mestic goddesses; it's about how Christian women point people
to God through their home. That is what accords with sound
doctrine—the gospel. Faithfulness in the practical matters of loving our husband and children and managing our homes honors
the gospel and shows the world the beauty of the gospel. We don't
manage our home because our home is our hope. We manage our
home because Christ is our hope.

Missional Motherhood Reaches from the Home to the World

Our missional motherhood starts in our Jerusalem (our homes, if you will), and extends outward from there to the outermost places of the world. We love our neighbor over in the next room first, starting with the ones rubbing peanut-butter handprints on our jeans or the ones ringing our phone off the hook during an emotional crisis. The rubber meets the road right where you're sitting. If you are a Christian, then you are a participant in the new creation by way of the death and resurrection of Jesus. He's given you his Spirit, who leads you to live in line with the truth of God's word. Our lives witness. They witness to our neighbors down the hall, in the grocery store, and in traffic, and they witness to the cosmic powers and principalities. Jesus is victorious over the grave! Look! Our faithfulness to these things is evidence that God, in his grace, is working out his new creation through us.

God's word helps remind us that missional motherhood is a strategic tool in the nail-scarred hands of the one who is summing up all things in himself. Jesus has ascended and has given his Spirit to those who are his. Look at all that Christ is yet doing in the world through their hands and through their feet and through their homes and all their ministries that reach out from inside the home to the outside world. Watch! And wonder! Don't forget: he is coming back. And when he does, he will render all accounts settled as he ushers in the fullness of his new creation and consummates his kingdom.

Conclusion

Missional Motherhood Is about a Man

We've had quite an adventure, haven't we? In the high-flying overview of the old, old story, God's pattern for nurturing life has been revealed, and we've seen his promises given. We've seen how we have been shown profound mercy—*life*! And amazing grace—*eternal life*! All those threads of redemptive history have been woven together to give us a glimpse of our Savior Jesus, who is mighty to save yet humble in heart. All our missional motherhood exists because of the cross and is played out in the shadow of the cross.

Sisters, we have much cause to rejoice today. God's grace *is* extending to more and more people. This is our labor of love to God and our neighbors: living to extend God's grace to more and more people, increasing thanksgiving to the glory of God (2 Cor. 4:15). Missional motherhood knows all too well that we are nurturing life in the face of death. As you have read this book, the overview of the Old Testament and the systematic way we've examined the person of Christ, I hope you can see more clearly how motherhood is about Jesus. The aim of all our mothering work is that his grace would extend to more and more people, increase thanksgiving to God, and glorify him (2 Cor. 4:15).

The Dramatic and Amazing End of Missional Motherhood

The good news of the gospel being offered freely to the nations as their only hope, and this being a way that he shows mercy "on all" (Rom. 11:32), is an unsearchable judgment and an inscrutable way of God. We can take confidence—steadying, flying-in-the-face-of-fear confidence—that God's plan of salvation through his Son Jesus will be accomplished by his Spirit. No doubt about it. If he can plan that kind of rescue for elect Israel and for the elect from every nation, then surely his hand will do it. He will bring it all to completion in the day of Christ, when he appears with the heavenly host in a blaze of glory. Can you imagine? This is why the idea of living missionally or having our motherhood be missional is far too great for us. *Mere* motherhood? Away with such an idea. God's plan of redemption and glorifying his Son through our nurturing of life is too lofty for us. But he has made it so, and we are thrilled at the prospect of serving our King in this way: "Declare his glory among the nations, his marvelous works among all the peoples!" (Ps. 96:3).

Dear reader, we are all part of all the nations. *Foreign* is relative. I mean, one time I was standing in a train station talking with a new acquaintance when she answered her mobile phone and told the person on the other line, "I'm talking with a foreigner." And here I was thinking that *I* was the one talking to a foreigner! We are all part of the nations, who are all accountable to God, so that means that he is Lord over you and me. He's the Lord over our kids and their kids and their kids. What he says he will do, his arm will surely do it. And the nations will be glad, and the nations will sing for joy (Ps. 67:4). His lost sheep *will* hear his voice, and they *will* follow him (John 10:27). Our neighbors are all on their way to eternity. Will we leverage our powerful ministry of missional motherhood for their eternal joy? We have *every* reason to be confident in the cause of missions and that our faith-fueled aim in missional motherhood will shake the very gates of hell, because

Christ is confident that he will receive worship, for he is the Lamb who was slain for us and was exalted above every name.

There is an appointed day for the end of our missional motherhood. It will be done. All the scurrying about we do in our daily work is but a fraction of the urgency that hangs over that day. The day is coming soon when the Son of Man is going to come with his angels in the glory of his Father (Matt. 16:27). What a day of rejoicing this will be for those from every tribe, tongue, and people group who eagerly wait for Christ's return! And what a day of distress it will be for all those found outside of Christ. Until that day, God's message of peace through Christ rings in our ears and sets our hearts ablaze. In grace-empowered love, we live on mission, imploring our children and our neighbors to repent of their sin and worship the Lamb who was slain for them, so they might taste and see that God is good.

May more and more of our neighbors from next door to across the globe join us as we sing the everlasting song to the praise of God's glory *forever*.

> Salvation belongs to our God who sits on the throne, and to the Lamb! (Rev. 7:10)

Would we learn to make much of Christ in our bedrooms, around our dining tables, on our Facebook walls, in our children's schools, in the waiting room at the doctor's office, in foreign lands, and *anywhere* that Jesus would be pleased to send us.

Missional Motherhood Is Not for the Faint of Heart
If we claim that we have been given the ministry of reconciliation, then we would do well to enjoy that reconciliation, study that reconciliation, revel in that reconciliation, and rest deeply in that reconciliation. If we have little joy in Christ, how can we share it with the people sitting around our breakfast table, much less the people in the rescue mission downtown or the orphanage across the ocean? Out of the *overflow* of that joy in Christ, we plead

with our children, we plead with the mom in the apartment next door, and in the means we are given, we plead with fellow sinners across the globe,

> Friend, what will you do with your sin? Where will you find true and lasting hope and peace? Come with me. Come to the cross with me. We need him! How we all so desperately need him! "For Christ is the end of the law for righteousness to everyone who believes" (Rom. 10:4). "Come, see a man. . . . Can this be the Christ?" (John 4:29). "The Spirit and the Bride say, 'Come.' And let the one who hears say, 'Come.' And let the one who is thirsty come; let the one who desires take the water of life without price" (Rev. 22:17). Be reconciled to God through Christ. There is no other way. Won't you come with me to Jesus?

No "just a mom" creature could utter such words. Only one given the cosmos-moving ministry of reconciliation can wield words like that.

You may have read on a greeting card somewhere that motherhood is not for the faint of heart. Don't believe it. Motherhood *has* to be for the faint of heart. Motherhood is mission: Jesus calls and equips women to discipleship—following him as he brings about the spreading of the glory of God in every corner of the earth. In his Great Commission, Jesus called you and every disciple to go and send, even if the farthest you go is to the nursery and back. You are on mission, and your labors are unto the Lord. Some women travel farther with the gospel and sacrifice even their very lives. If we take a peek into church history, we see that missional mothers are even among the elect martyrs of the church. Did you know that time would fail us if we were to speak of the testimonies of such women? Read about women like Lucia, Blandina, Perpetua, Betty Stam, and Betty Olsen, and imitate their faith. Even today, women are among those who lose their lives for the witness they bear, and their souls cry out from under the altar of God with a loud voice, "O Sovereign Lord, holy and true, how long before you will judge and avenge our blood on those who dwell on the earth?" (Rev. 6:10). May God strengthen our faith to proclaim his good news in the face of death and a million deaths to self.

A million deaths to self still add up to a million. This kind of motherhood can be only for the faint of heart, and Jesus proves to be the only sustenance for us. As Russell Moore, president of the Ethics and Religious Liberty Commission, wrote in an article decrying the abortion industry in America, "The presence of the weak, the vulnerable, and the dependent is a matter of spiritual warfare."[35] We might not lose our lives for the sake of the gospel, but we may be called to gladly sacrifice our comfort, excess, and reputation in order to nurture the physical and spiritual lives of the weak, vulnerable, and dependent. As we make those sacrifices, we remember that we are not wrestling against flesh and blood when we preserve life both inside and outside the womb. We are not wrestling against flesh and blood at any point in our womanly, nurturing work. They may say you are *just* feeding a hungry child, *just* filling out paperwork, *just* folding laundry, or *just* paying the bills. But we know there is no *just* about nurturing life in the face of death. God gives us his own spiritual armor (Eph. 6:10–18) to aid us as we labor to be pro–all the life he creates, to preserve our faith, and to defend us from satanic oppression as we endure ridicule and persecution for nurturing life at every juncture (especially the most vulnerable lives among us) in our home, workplace, neighborhood, and world. Incidentally, this spiritual armor fits even over maternity elastic.[36]

There is much work to be done and many people to be loved. There's no way we can do this on our own. Moms have to be strengthened by grace to make the necessary sacrifices and to do the mundane, routine things that move the gospel forward. Few celebrities are likely to invite you onto their shows to shower you with gifts for praying with your kids, organizing a baby shower for a single mom, visiting a missionary, sending letters to your lawmaking representatives, or discipling the teen girls in your church. Only Jesus knows how many faith-full women have labored in his Great Commission behind the scenes in these ways. And he knows how many more missional mothers he will raise up to serve him with all the nurturing strength he provides. I hope you are encouraged, dear reader, that Jesus is building up his body through the work of women who are mobilizing missionaries, teaching the Bible, extending hospitality, reaching out to the suffering, and doing a host of other good works.

The world says that you are *just* a mom and that your mothering ministry is not newsworthy. The world says your work is mundane, but every mothering and discipling moment in your life is actually unique—unprecedented in history and never to be repeated. Your work in evangelism and discipleship done through the power of the Spirit gives Jesus praise that echoes in eternity. And this moves heaven to rejoice.

How Jesus Leads Moms on Mission

Missional motherhood is a way of life that overflows from your heart for the gospel. We all need grace for our missional motherhood. A life lived on biblical mission is characterized by Spirit-empowered dying to self as one overflows in grace to others, compelled by the love of Christ (2 Cor. 5:14). But we are sinners who live in a fallen world, and we get distracted, discouraged, and disenfranchised. The problem we have with living on mission is neither the mission nor the message; the problem lies with our sin. Our biggest problem is not that we lack the resources or creativity or ideas or planning for missional living. Our biggest problem is our sin.

Missional motherhood has no real message of any kind of lasting hope unless we have the gospel. We have every reason to rejoice because the problem of our sin has been completely, totally, utterly dealt with on the cross of Jesus Christ. In order to lead us in his cause of nurturing life and giving eternal life to whom he will, Jesus must first deliver us out of death. Jesus has rescued us from the wrath of God:

> For if while we were enemies we were reconciled to God by the death of his Son, much more, now that we are reconciled, shall we be saved by his life. (Rom. 5:10)

Jesus defeated death:

> If the Spirit of him who raised Jesus from the dead dwells in you, he who raised Christ Jesus from the dead will also give life to your mortal bodies through his Spirit who dwells in you. (Rom. 8:11)

Jesus took away our sin in his own body:

> He himself bore our sins in his body on the tree, that we might die to sin and live to righteousness. By his wounds you have been healed. (1 Pet. 2:24)

Jesus makes our dead souls come alive:

> Even when we were dead in our trespasses, [God] made us alive together with Christ—by grace you have been saved. (Eph. 2:5)

Jesus spares us alienation from God and gives us his Spirit to dwell in us:

> . . . even the Spirit of truth, whom the world cannot receive, because it neither sees him nor knows him. You know him, for he dwells with you and will be in you. (John 14:17)

> And behold, I am with you always, to the end of the age. (Matt. 28:20)

Jesus gives us his own righteousness, because without righteousness we cannot stand before a holy God blameless forever and ever:

> For our sake he made him to be sin who knew no sin, so that in him we might become the righteousness of God. (2 Cor. 5:21)

Friend, do you believe this? Does your faith in this Christ shape the way you look at your role as a mom and a discipler? Do thoughts of his cross give you hope and strength? Oh, friend! I hope so. You and I have every reason to flee from our sin, cling to Jesus's cross, and take up our cross on mission as we follow Christ. Jesus is both willing and able to carry us all the way home. It was his plan from the beginning, from before time, and it is all from him at every point. See how the Bible describes in a short sentence our ministry:

> All this is from God, who through Christ reconciled us to himself and gave us the ministry of reconciliation. (2 Cor. 5:18)

When we see ourselves in need of grace, and when we see that our children and disciples are also in need of grace because they are just like us, then we can hold out the cross as our answer for everything because it was Jesus's answer for everything. Now nothing stands in the way of our enjoyment of God forever. Let's run together with him wherever he leads us while we are yet alive on this earth. The time is now for us to take up his Great Commission and let it transform our motherhood into mission.

Notes

1. Westminster Shorter Catechism, Question 4.
2. This thought comes from a quote by John Piper, which is expounded upon in this article: http://www.desiringgod.org/articles /every-moment-in-2013-god-will-be-doing-10-000-things-in-your-life.
3. "Cast all your anxiety on him because he cares for you."
4. Disclaimer: My friend Theresa reported that she read "Jesus Has Written Us into His Story" in fifteen minutes, and she is a fast reader. Please accept my apologies if your coffee gets too cold to drink by the time you're done reading this section!
5. Jim Hamilton has written a helpful and readable guide to understanding biblical theology. I highly recommend starting with his book if you would like to read a compact work about the unified story of the Bible. *What Is Biblical Theology?: A Guide to the Bible's Story, Symbolism, and Patterns* (Wheaton, IL: Crossway, 2014).
6. Westminster Shorter Catechism, Q. 9.
7. Ibid., Q. 10.
8. G. K. Beale, *The Temple and the Church's Mission: A Biblical Theology of the Dwelling Place of God* (Downers Grove, IL: IVP Academic, 2004), n.p.
9. Elisabeth Elliot, testimony at Urbana conference, 1996. You can watch video of her sharing her testimony at https://www.youtube.com/watch ?v=0Q4X_DOT0d0.
10. J. I. Packer, *Evangelism and the Sovereignty of God* (Downers Grove, IL: InterVarsity, 1991), 11–12.
11. "Accordingly, 1 Kings 3:9 is likely one more way to depict Solomon as an Adam figure." G. K. Beale, *A New Testament Biblical Theology: The Unfolding of the Old Testament in the New* (Ada, MI: Baker Academic, 2011), 69.
12. Gen. 2:15, 19–20.
13. Packer, *Evangelism and the Sovereignty of God*, 73.
14. Beale, *New Testament Biblical Theology*, 203.

15. Josephus, *Wars of the Jews*, 1:141.

16. Placide Cappeau de Roquemaure, "O Holy Night" (1847).

17. Packer, *Evangelism and the Sovereignty of God*, 33.

18. John Piper has exquisitely explained this in his book *Desiring God: Meditations of a Christian Hedonist*, rev. and exp. (Colorado Springs, CO: Multnomah, 2003). And in every other book he has ever written.

19. Janet and Amy are not their real names.

20. Shai Linne, "The Perfection of Beauty," in *The Attributes of God* album, Lamp Mode Recordings, 2011.

21. Robert Lowry, "Nothing but the Blood," 1876.

22. "How Firm a Foundation," attributed to "K," in *A Selection of Hymns from the Best Authors,* comp. John Rippon, 1787.

23. Just to illustrate this, here are a few stats: less than 2 percent of Old Testament prophecy is messianic, less than 5 percent refers to our new-covenant era, and less than 1 percent is about events that are yet to come.

24. Susan Hunt, *Spiritual Mothering: The Titus 2 Model for Mentoring Women* (Wheaton, IL: Crossway, 1992), 15.

25. "How Firm a Foundation," attributed to "K."

26. For an outstanding resource on discerning God's will and sound counsel against the popular admonition to "follow your heart," please see Kevin DeYoung's book *Just Do Something: A Liberating Approach to Finding God's Will* (Chicago, IL: Moody, 2009).

27. This phrase comes from the title of chapter 20 in the third volume of John Calvin's *Institutes of the Christian Religion* (1536).

28. Martyn Lloyd-Jones, *Preaching and Preachers* (Grand Rapids, MI: Zondervan, 1972), 170–71.

29. David Platt, *Radical: Taking Your Faith Back from the American Dream* (Colorado Springs, CO: Multnomah, 2010), 216.

30. Hara Estroff Marano, "Helicopter Parenting—It's Worse Than You Think," *Psychology Today* website, https://www.psychologytoday.com /blog/nation-wimps/201401/helicopter-parenting-its-worse-you-think.

31. Tim Keesee, "No Regrets, No Retreat," Episode 8, *Dispatches from the Front* DVD series. This excellent series is available at http://www.front linemissions/info.

32. C. S. Lewis, *The Weight of Glory* (New York: HarperOne, 2001), 45–46.

33. I have adapted this line from a quote in J. I. Packer's book *Evangelism and the Sovereignty of God*, 40. "Evangelism is man's work, but the giving of the faith is God's."

34. For more on this concept, see David Sitton, *Reckless Abandon: A Gospel Pioneer's Exploits Among the Most Difficult to Reach Peoples*, 2nd ed. (Greenville, SC: Ambassador International, 2013).

35. Russell Moore, "Planned Parenthood vs. Jesus Christ," Moore to the Point blog, August 4, 2015, http://www.russellmoore.com/2015/08/04 /planned-parenthood-vs-jesus-christ/.

36. In an article entitled "A Pregnant Woman's Defense against the Schemes of the Devil," Desiring God blog (May 26, 2012), I argue that the spiritual armor passage in Ephesians 6:10–18 is particularly pertinent to pregnant women who are considering the issues in the cultural "Mommy Wars." http://www.desiringgod.org/articles /a-pregnant-woman-s-defense-against-the-schemes-of-the-devil.

General Index

Abraham and Sarah, 32, 33, 52–53
Adam, 30
Adam and Eve, 30, 31, 32, 47, 173

Bible, 28; unity of its message, 40–41
Boaz, 34

children, timing of ordained by God, 173
church, in Dubai, 16, 22–23; follows Jesus, 160; a priestly ministry, 159
covenant, 32, 52
Cretans, 186–88
creation, 44; new, 37
cross, shadow of in Old Testament, 30, 40; answer for everything, 200

David, 34
Devil. *See* Satan.
discipleship of women, 172, 179–80, 196
Dubai, 16, church in, 22–23

evangelism as mom's work, 175
Eve, 50

gender, differences of, 109–10
God, breath of (*ruah*), 44–46; image of, 15; instructions of, 33; mission of, 15, 33–37; and motherhood, 89; praise of, 176; promises of, 31, 34, 177; story of, 29
"good works," 188–89
gospel, the, 36, 129; of grace, 112; hope of, 25; need to share, 36, 120–21, 172
Great Commission, 171

Hezekiah, 150; prayer of intercession, 150–51
Holy Spirit, facilitates prayer, 161
home, managing of, 190; as ministry, 185–86; "Titus 2" home, 185–86, 190; as witness, 191
hope, 25, 32
human beings, as creatures, 42–44; purpose of, 45

Scripture Index

214   *Scripture Index*

1:11–14	126
1:16	41
1:17	43
1:21–23	123
2:8	144
3:1–4	185

1 Thessalonians

2:4	70
4:7	123
5:1–11	140

2 Thessalonians

| 2:7 | 95 |

1 Timothy

| 5:3–14 | 188 |

2 Timothy

2:13	81
3:1–9	138
3:16–17	45, 189
4:3–4	138

Titus

1:10–11	186
1:10–16	186
1:12	187
1:13	187
1:16	187
2	185–190
2:1	187
2:2–5	187
2:7	188
2:10	187, 188
2:11	14
2:11–14	189–90
2:13	128

2:13–14	189
3:8	189
3:14	189

Hebrews

1:1–2	135
7	152, 155
7:16	155
7:21	156
7:22–25	157
7:27	64
8	152
8:1–2	153
8:5	60
9:11–24	62
9:12	64
9:13–14	157
9:26	64
10:1	64
10:4	149
10:12–14	158
11:16	78
12:2	127
12:14	158
12:22–24	159
12:24	94
13:12–16	160

James

| 4:2 | 162 |

1 Peter

1:18–19	69
1:23	53
2:5	152, 159
2:9	140
2:24	199
5:7	23

Also Available from Gloria Furman

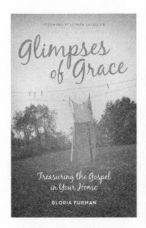

For more information, visit **crossway.org**.